THE OPEN CLASSROOM

THE OPEN CLASSROOM

A Practical Guide to
A New Way of Teaching

HERBERT R. KOHL

A New York Review Book

Distributed by Vintage Books,
A Division of Random House, Inc.

A NEW YORK REVIEW BOOK
Distributed by Vintage Books,
A Division of Random House, Inc.

Published by The New York Review,
250 West 57th Street
New York, New York 10019

First Printing, November 1969
Second Printing, January 1970
Third Printing, March 1970
Fourth Printing, June 1970
Fifth Printing, September 1970
Sixth Printing, February 1971
Seventh Printing, August 1971
Eighth Printing, October 1971
Ninth Printing, June 1972
Tenth Printing, October 1972
Eleventh Printing, August 1973
Twelfth Printing, April 1974
Thirteenth Printing, February 1977

Printed in the U.S.A.
ISBN 0–394–70614–5

Contents

	Introduction	9
I	Beginning the School Year	15
II	Planning and Lesson Plans	46
III	Some Classrooms in Operation	55
IV	Ten Minutes a Day	66
V	Discipline	74
VI	Troubles with Principals, Assistant Principals, and Other Supervisors	86
VII	Problems	94
VIII	Conclusions	111

Dedication

To the people I have learned from and especially to: Ronald Evans; Charlie Carter; Leroy Carter; Zelda Wirtschafter; Joel Ziff; Ted Koptchek; Carol Morel, Ted Morgan, Susan Rizzo and their classes; John Rosenbaum; Jim Herndon, Raymond Ryder; Robert Maynard; my theater class at Berkeley High School; all the people at Other Ways, I.S. 201, *What's Happening;* the students at Columbia, Berkeley, Ann Arbor, El Cerito, Orinda; and of course to Judy, Tonia, and Erica.

Introduction

When I began teaching I felt isolated in a hostile environment. The structure of authority in my school was clear: the principal was at the top and the students were at the bottom. Somewhere in the middle was the teacher, whose role it was to impose orders from textbooks or supervisors upon the students. The teacher's only protection was that if students failed to obey instructions they could legitimately be punished or, if they were defiant, suspended or kicked out of school. There was no way for students to question the teachers' decisions or for teachers to question the decisions of their supervisors or authors of textbooks and teachers' manuals.

My school happened to be in a black ghetto in New York City, and I thought for a while that it was a pathological case. In the last few years I have spoken with many teachers throughout the country and visited many schools—urban, suburban, black, white, integrated, segregated, elementary, secondary. There is the same obsession with power and discipline everywhere; for most American children there is essentially one public school system in the United

States, and it is authoritarian and oppressive. Students everywhere are deprived of the right to make choices concerning their own destinies. My experiences in a Harlem elementary school were not special, and I think the discoveries I made about myself and my students apply to most schools.

The authoritarian environment of the school I taught at encouraged a collusive atmosphere in which everyone except the students pretended that the school was functioning smoothly and effectively and that the teachers were "doing a good job." It was not proper to talk about troubles or admit failures.

There was no one for me to talk with, to share my despair and confusion. I was having troubles with the curriculum, with my students, with bureaucratic details, with other teachers, and, most of all, with myself. I was bewildered and angered by what was expected of me, and overwhelmed by my contact with students. I was supposed to teach the fifth-grade curriculum, no matter who my students were or what they cared about. I was also supposed to take attendance; sign circulars; contribute to a fund for purchasing birthday presents for colleagues who refused to acknowledge my existence; take my turn at yard duty, hall duty, and lunchroom duty. The demands were as frequent as they were senseless. Yet they were insignificant when compared with the pressure to fulfill the function considered most essential to a teacher's success—controlling the children.

The entire staff of the school was obsessed by "control," and beneath the rhetoric of faculty meetings was the clear implication that students were a reckless, unpredictable, immoral, and dangerous enemy.

I found myself following the usual methods. The textbooks bored me; yet I went along and tried to impose them upon my students. The clerical work seemed to me absurd, yet with my students I tried to make it seem important. They weren't impressed, and because I didn't have the heart to harass them, they mocked and harassed me. My students hated school and let me know it by running about the room, screaming, falling out of their seats. There were a few times when something developed in the classroom that led the students to become absorbed in learning. Yet for the most part I was having trouble, and I wanted to talk to someone about it. In the authoritarian atmosphere of the school no one wanted to hear about my troubles—if the system didn't work in my case, I probably wasn't suited to the job.

After a few months of teaching, however, I met another teacher in my school who spoke honestly about teaching. His class was a wonder to me—the atmosphere was open, there was a casual and friendly exchange between him and his pupils. This absence of hostility was accompanied by the intense involvement of the students in things they seemed to care about. What he had achieved seemed unattainable for me, given the state of my class. I couldn't believe that he had ever confronted problems with students or had ever been uncertain about his role in the classroom. But we talked about my problems and he told me of his own difficulties during his early years as a teacher. Knowing that he had similar problems made me somewhat more hopeful. He helped me to locate the source of my difficulties in myself and in the pathology of the classroom instead of in the students. He

also showed me the need to find alternatives to textbooks and to the domination of the teacher.

That first six months I just managed to survive.
The next year was much better and I learned how to
make the classroom more interesting for my pupils. I
also learned how to give up my power as a teacher
(not delegate it but abrogate it) and how to help my
pupils as well as become someone they could talk
with. I learned to listen to them, to be led by their
interests and needs. In turn I became involved in
creating things in the classroom—in doing research
on myths and numbers, in learning from the experience of the students. My students and I resembled
a community much more than a class, and I en-
joyed being with them. We worked together in an
open environment which often spilled out of the
school building into the streets, the neighborhood,
and the city itself.

Yet these things didn't happen magically or
quickly. I needed a great deal of help, and very little
was available. I did learn to function in a non-authoritarian way within an authoritarian institution, though
I had little impact on the school, and ultimately quit.
Still I gradually found ways of teaching that were not
based on compulsion but on participation; not on
grades or tests or curriculum, but on pursuing what
interested the children.

Other teachers are going through the same process
of yielding some of their authority and freeing themselves to teach without using compulsion. Many have
been fired for trying to teach in non-authoritarian
ways; others have been trying to change and finding
themselves confused or impatient. It is difficult to

yield power and develop a sense of community with young people (or even with one's peers, for that matter).

This book is a handbook for teachers who want to work in an open environment. It is difficult to say exactly what an open classroom is. One almost has to have been in one and feel what it is. However there are certain things that it is not. It is important not to equate an open classroom with a "permissive" environment. In an open classroom the teacher must be as much himself as the pupils are themselves. This means that if the teacher is angry he ought to express his anger, and if he is annoyed at someone's behavior he ought to express that, too. In an authoritarian classroom annoying behavior is legislated out of existence. In a "permissive" classroom the teacher pretends it isn't annoying. He also permits students to behave only in certain ways, thereby retaining the authority over their behavior he pretends to be giving up. In an open situation the teacher tries to express what he feels and to deal with each situation as a communal problem.

This book is based upon the experience of teachers: their problems, failures, and frustrations, as well as their successes. It is about the battles with self and system that teachers encounter in the schools. But it is not a handbook that gives teachers a step-by-step account of how to change their classrooms and themselves. Each teacher must obviously go through the process of change in ways consistent with his own personality. This handbook does, however, try to anticipate problems, to present possibilities and make suggestions. It presents some strategies for change, for dealing with the administration and other teachers, for creating different kinds of textbooks, lesson plans, etc. It can and I hope will be used by different people in different ways.

This book is primarily addressed to public school teachers. However, much is I think relevant to other teachers in community schools, in private schools, and at colleges and universities. Power is a problem for all of us. The development of open, democratic modes of existence is essentially the problem of abandoning the authoritarian use of power and of providing workable alternatives. That is a problem that must be faced by all individuals and institutions that presume to teach.

I

Beginning the
School Year

Expectations

Teachers begin the school year burdened with expectations and preconceptions that often interfere with the development of open classrooms. Classes are "tracked" and students are placed together according to academic achievement. Reading achievement or I.Q. scores are usually used to decide which track a student "belongs" in, though sometimes teachers' judgments about their students' potential count too. There are top, middle, and bottom classes; A, B, C, and D "streams." No matter how schools try to conceal this grouping, the pupils know where they are placed. Bottom classes, the C and D streams, often tell their teachers at the beginning of the school year, "You can't expect much from us. We're dumb."

Teachers know the type of class they are expected to be teaching.[1] Before the teacher has even met his

---

[1] In some Union contracts there are even provisions for rotation of teachers from top to bottom, through the middle to the top again.

students his expectations of bright, mediocre, or dull individuals are set.

Even in schools which have abandoned tracking, the teacher is given a set of record cards by his supervisor which document the child's school life as perceived by his previous teachers. These cards usually contain achievement and I.Q. scores, personality evaluations, descriptions of conferences with the students' parents, judgments about his behavior in class and "study habits." Difficult pupils are identified as well as good (i.e., conforming and performing) ones. The record cards are probably designed not only as analyses of their pupils' careers at school, but as warnings to teachers on what to expect.

When the teacher meets his class on the first day of the school year, he is armed with all of this "professional" knowledge. Anticipating a dull class, for example, a teacher may have spent several weeks preparing simple exercises to keep his students busy. On the other hand, faced with the prospect of teaching a bright class, he may have found a new and challenging textbook or devised some ingenious scientific experiments.

If the record cards indicate that several pupils are particularly troublesome or, what is more threatening, "disturbed," the teacher will single them out as soon as they enter the room and treat them differently from the other pupils. He may do the same with bright students or ones rumored to be wise, funny, lazy, violent, scheming, deceitful. . . . The students will sense this and act in the manner expected of them. Thus the teacher traps both himself and his pupils into repeating patterns that have been set for years.

Expectations influence behavior in subtle ways: a successful though nervous and unhappy student may try to relax. His teacher says, "What's the matter? You're not yourself this week." This may produce feelings of guilt in the student, who then drives himself to succeed in spite of feeling that the price he is paying for academic achievement may be excessive.

A "difficult" student tries to make a new start and is quiet and obedient. His teacher responds to this behavior by saying, "You're off to a good start this year," and so informs the student that a bad start was expected of him. The student becomes angry and defiant.

A supposedly dull student gives a correct answer in class and is praised excessively. He is embarrassed and becomes withdrawn.

Even in kindergarten a teacher will have expectations. Some children are "disadvantaged," others have language problems. The teacher anticipates that they may not do well. Others come from intellectual or privileged homes and if they don't perform well something must be wrong.

Teachers' expectations have a tendency to become self-fulfilling.[2] "Bad" classes tend to act badly, and "gifted" classes tend to respond to the special consideration that they expect to be given to them if they perform in a "superior" way.

All of this is inimical to an open classroom, where the role of the teacher is not to control his pupils but

---

[2] For a study of self-fulfilling prophecies, see *Pygmalion in the Classroom: Teacher Expectation and the Pupil's Intellectual Ability,* by Robert Rosenthal and Lenore Jacobson, Holt, Rinehart & Winston, 1968, $4.95; $3.95 (paper).

rather to enable them to make choices and pursue what interests them. In an open classroom a pupil functions according to his sense of himself rather than what he is expected to be. It is not that the teacher should expect the same of all his pupils. On the contrary, the teacher must learn to perceive differences, but these should emerge from what actually happens in the classroom during the school year, and not from preconceptions.

I remember an incident where the effect of a teacher's expectations in one of my classes was pernicious. I have always been unable to avoid having favorites in my classes. I like defiant, independent, and humorous people, and my preferences naturally come out in my teaching. One year, several students were puzzled by my choice of favorites. The class had been together for three years and each year teachers chose the same four children as their favorite students. However, I had chosen different students and this upset most of the class, especially the ones who had been favorites in the past. All the students were black. It took me several months to realize that the former favorites were all the lightest-skinned pupils in the class—in other words, the whitest were (by their white teachers) expected to be the nicest and most intelligent.

A teacher in an open classroom needs to cultivate a state of *suspended expectations*. It is not easy. It is easy to believe that a dull class is dull, or a bright class is bright. The words "emotionally disturbed" conjure up frightening images. And it is sometimes a relief to discover that there are good pupils in the class that is waiting for you. Not reading the record cards or ignoring the standing of the class is an act of self-denial; it involves casting aside a crutch when one still believes one can't walk without it. Yet if one wants to develop an open classroom within the setting of a school which is essentially totalitarian, such acts of will are necessary.

What does it mean to suspend expectations when one is told that the class one will be teaching is slow, or bright, or ordinary? At the least it means not preparing to teach in any special way or deciding beforehand on the complexity of the materials to be used during a school year. It means that planning does not consist of finding the class's achievement level according to the record cards and tailoring the material to that level, but rather preparing diverse materials and subjects and discovering from the students as the year unfolds what is relevant to them and what isn't.

Particularly it means not reading I.Q. scores or achievement scores, not discovering who may be a source of trouble and who a solace or even a joy. It means giving your pupils a fresh chance to develop in new ways in your classroom, freed from the roles they may have adopted during their previous school careers. It means allowing children to become who they care to become, and freeing the teacher from the standards by which new pupils had been measured in the past.

There are no simple ways to give up deeply rooted expectations. There are some suggestions, however:

—talk to students outside class
—watch them play and watch them live with other young people

—play with them—joking games and serious
  games
—talk to them about yourself, what you care
  about
—listen

In these situations the kids may surprise you and
reveal rather than conceal, as is usual in the classroom, their feelings, playfulness, and intelligence.

The First Day of School

The students walk into the room the teacher has
been assigned. The school year has begun. Usually
the class sits down before the teacher makes his first
remarks. Sometimes the class stands up, waiting.
Whatever happens, the first move of the school year
is the teacher's.

He introduces himself, calls the roll of pupils'
names (usually in alphabetical order), and then assigns seats.

The assignment of seats, perhaps the first act the
teacher performs during the school year, can stand
symbolically for many things that occur in authoritarian classrooms. It is the teacher who assigns the
seats and the pupils who must obey. Even in those
few classes where the pupils are allowed to choose
their seats it is usually made clear that once chosen,
the seats can't be changed.

Usually the order of seating is quite arbitrary—according to the size and sex of pupils or by alphabetical order. The primary function of this order seems to be to provide the teacher with an immediate way of knowing where his pupils are so they can't put anything over on him before he learns their names. During the course of the year the teacher adjusts the seating according to his convenience or need, isolating troublemakers, rewarding good pupils, etc. But it is always the teacher who commands.

An open classroom is different. Pupils are free to choose and change their seats. So is the teacher. When disputes arise they must be adjudicated and finally settled with all parties involved. If two people want the same seat they must settle it with each other and with the teacher and with other pupils. There is, of course, no formula for resolving all conflicts. It is a matter of learning how to bargain and compromise. But one must make sure that an authoritarian structure controlled by pupils does not replace the one the teacher has refused to impose. This is a difficult and delicate matter.

Young people in American schools are used to authoritarian methods. They experience them in school, in their families, and in society at large. They cannot be expected to fit into a more open situation without misgivings and without, in some circumstances, assuming the authoritarian roles their teachers have abdicated. They are used to controlling or being controlled and will often be harder on each other than are the most oppressive adults.

Children playing school can be incredibly cruel. I remember watching a group of nine- and ten-year-old girls playing school. The "teacher" had a stick and she was whacking the other girls, screaming at them, forcing them to spell words out loud, and berating them for always being wrong. It took me quite a while to realize that correct spelling was irrelevant to the game since neither the "teacher" nor her "pupils" knew or cared about the correct spelling of words. They were acting out the role of the omniscient teacher and the ignorant pupil. For them being a teacher meant exercising control and being a pupil meant being submissive.

Yet a classroom can become more democratic. People can come to listen to each other and care about each other's thoughts and feelings. It takes patience, and a belief in the potential of the children. Time must be taken, especially in the beginning of the school year, to work out disputes over seating and other seemingly petty things like hanging up coats, lining up, and going in and out of the school building. When these are done without specific directions and without imposing sanctions against offenders, some disputes are bound to arise. That is the price of developing a democratic classroom where pupils and teacher find ways of functioning together without invoking arbitrary or absolute authority.

I have seen the most defeated students, the ones most thoroughly oppressed in school, coming back year after year, looking fresh and open on the first day of school, ready to put their failure and despair and cynicism aside and begin again, if only it were made possible for them to do so.

Presenting One's Self in the Classroom

How can a teacher present the prospect of a free classroom to pupils who have for years been used to doing what they are told in school? What does one say to the class after they are seated and what does one do that first day? Must one establish control first and then gradually give the class freedom, or can a classroom be free and open from the start?

Usually the first day of class is used to familiarize the students with the routines and rules the teacher intends to impose upon the class throughout the year. After the teacher has introduced himself and assigned seats, he then tells the students what to expect in his class. The "do's" and "don'ts" are paraded out. Don't leave your seat without permission; don't talk out; do raise your hand if you want something; do remain quiet at the beginning of class; don't chew gum. . . . Often these rules are codified and posted above the chalk board in the front of the room. Most frequently they refer to behavior and what is euphemistically referred to as work habits, i.e., penmanship, the use of proper headings, the absence of erasures, etc. Sometimes they refer to dress. Often these codes are written in pseudo democratic style using the royal "we" to proclaim, for example, that "we always raise our hands when we want to say something." What is meant is the students must raise their hands to be recognized by the teacher before they can legitimately talk in the classroom.

After announcing the class code, the teacher sets to work on establishing routines. This is especially true in elementary schools where students may spend as much as five hours a day in the same room. The routines range from procedures for entering and leaving the room, using the toilets, passing out and collecting papers, and sharpening pencils, to methods of lining up and hanging up coats in an orderly fashion. It is amazing how much time can be filled by these procedural matters, and how useful they can be for a teacher who insists that the first order of business during the school year is to establish an orderly and controlled classroom. From the very first day the students know the range and scope of movement and expression allowed them in the classroom. They know what acts will be punished and what conformity and defiance mean for that particular teacher. It makes it easier for those students who choose to acquiesce in the authoritarian structure to develop routines of their own which offer them maximum freedom within the structure imposed upon them. They know what they can "get away with."

The Student Underworld

If you have spent a number of years at the same school, the students know all about your style without having to be in your class. The student underground has probably checked you out and delivered a verdict to the school.

Students talk to one another about teachers and have their own criteria for judging them. I remember passing on information about my teachers when I was in school and have heard my pupils doing the same thing. Our criteria for judging teachers were the same, though our school careers were at least fifteen years apart.

Good teachers, according to students, are generally the ones who are fair, do not lie, and are easy to talk to. Strictness is not necessarily a defect. An honest but strict teacher is often considered difficult but worth having. A soft teacher is often made fun of. Students make subtle distinctions between teachers who are open because they believe in a free spirit in the classroom, on the one hand, and those who are "easy" because they are afraid of the confrontation they may provoke if they assert authority.

Arbitrary and authoritarian teachers are considered enemies. Students warn one another about them and go out of their way to disrupt and defy these teachers.

It is essential to listen to the voice of the students. They are not afraid to talk about what actually happens in school.

Rules and Routines

It is difficult for beginning teachers to establish control because they have not yet sensed that control comes as much through imposing rules and routines as it does from the personal authority of the teacher. Not having had a class of their own yet, they can't imagine the degree to which routine (and not curriculum, not learning, not teaching) can be used to control and contain the behavior of students. When my wife first taught, she was overwhelmed by the number of things she had to do that seemed to have nothing to do with teaching. She had to call the roll; line up her pupils; organize fire drills; pass out and collect papers, books, and pencils; lead the pledge to the flag; collect milk and lunch money, and so on. Failing to perceive how these extraneous activities contributed to maintaining control in the classroom, she was exasperated. A second-year teacher, sensing her frustration, reassured her that after the first year it wasn't so bad. "In fact," she said, "after the first year teaching is just like being a secretary." Once you get your routines straight you can control space and time in your environment. The content or quality of what you are doing is irrelevant.

It is not only routines and rules that shore up the authoritarian classroom. Textbooks and workbooks have the same function. The first year it may be difficult to get the knack of using them, but after that one can do the same thing year after year—read the same stories, ask the same questions, get the same answers. It may get boring but it also gets easier. Chance occurrences are minimized.

In an open classroom it is different. Each school year is unique for both the students and the teacher. The first day is not filled with the mastery of routines and the pronouncement of rules. It is not possible to anticipate which rules or routines will emerge as convenient or necessary for a particular class. Nor is it desirable to announce rigid rules and routines when they may prove irrelevant or cumbersome later in the year, and one may want to abandon them. Just as one has to suspend expectations with respect to individual students, so with respect to rules and routines one must suspend one's fear of chaos.

One must face one's fear that young people will run wild if they are not held down or controlled. The spectre of chaos haunts many teachers, probably because they don't believe in their own strength or ability to handle the power they assume. Yet there is no need to impose rules or pull rank. It is possible to assume that rules and routines are necessary only as they emerge as indispensable for the group's functioning. If students find ways to line up and sit down, hang up their coats, choose and change their seats with a minimum of problems, why bother to restrict them by rigid routines? If discussion can develop without the students raising their hands, why bother with that procedure? As teachers are more willing to take chances with new ways of acting they may find it increasingly possible to be themselves and relax with young people.

However, hanging up coats in the morning, for example, may become a real problem if students fight over hooks or take things from each other's pockets or throw coats on the floor. In these circumstances something must be done—the problem can't be ignored without destroying respect for the teacher as an honest and strong person. But that does not mean that the teacher should legislate the problem of coats out of existence. The people in the class must deal with it as their problem and come to some resolution.

The students involved can, for example, settle the matter in private with the teacher adjudicating. The problem can also be settled by the class in a general discussion or a mock trial. There are theatrical and playful ways to deal with the problem of coathooks too. The teacher can suggest that the whole class try to hang their coats on one hook, or do without hooks for a day, or find other places in the classroom to store their coats. Then the question of storing coats can be discussed in a general way or in relationship to the coat games. The initial incident can be forgotten or made to seem insignificant.

All this may take time—time that will be taken away from reading and science and social studies and other supposedly basic work. One must learn to respond to what happens spontaneously in the classroom and to put aside one's other plans. This is as true with matters of curriculum as with "discipline" problems. For example, a short story may refer to an earthquake in passing and the class may be more interested in discussing earthquakes than in finishing the story. Or in studying motion in physics some students may want to look into motion in dance or track. A math lesson on probability theory can lead to a crap game and even to a historical study of the origins of dice. A discussion of the French Revolution can lead by association to a study of instruments of execution, of penal institutions, and finally the role of law in an unjust society. A teacher has to learn to go with the class, to respond to their desire to learn about things and not cut off their enthusiasm in the service of getting through the curriculum. It is necessary to take time to solve problems communally. The democratic development of routines and rules and restrictions is as crucial to the development of freedom in an open classroom as the arbitrary imposition of them is central to control in an authoritarian class.

The concept of order in an open classroom is not the same as that current in the schools where rules and routines are developed to avoid disagreements. In most classrooms there is no place for argument or conflict, nor is there time for teachers and pupils to learn how to live with and listen to each other. There is no give-and-take. The students direct their talk to the teacher, and obey the teacher's rules. Conflict, defiance, or disagreement are disciplinary problems and offenders must be punished. In an open classroom there is considerable give-and-take, argument, disagreement, even conflict. These are organic elements in the life of the group, to be dealt with and resolved by the group and arbitrated by the teacher.

The teacher is a mediator and not a judge or executioner.

Students may have disputes about where they want to sit, or how to line up. It may take a while for them to learn to talk or listen to each other or to the teacher. But in the classroom—as in life—it is more dangerous to legislate disagreement out of existence than to accept and integrate it into the whole.

The first day of school does not have to consist of proclaiming rules and practicing routines. There are other things a teacher can do on the first day. It depends upon his style and personality, the subject he is teaching, the age of the students—any number of things. The important point, however, is that in an open classroom the teacher is no more required to behave like a "teacher" than the students are required to be submissive children. The teacher needn't always be at the front of the room and lead, nor does he have to speak "proper" English, nor defend a rigid system of "right" and "wrong." He can be in the classroom the same complex person he is in life and relieve himself of the strain of assuming what he thinks to be the appropriate persona. He needn't be afraid of the students learning his first name, nor of talking with the class about his "private" life and experiences, his confusions, defeats, and triumphs. He can use his own experiences to help his students deal with theirs.

Often on the first day students are asked to write an essay on themselves, or a theme on "what I did last summer." Such assignments may be well intentioned, but they miss something crucial. The students are asked to write about themselves and their experiences. What about the teacher? Shouldn't the students have as much opportunity to assess the teacher's words as he theirs? One way of beginning a school year is by telling the pupils about yourself—where you came from, where you are, and where you think you are going. Then it may make more sense to the students to talk of themselves in reasonably open and honest ways.

Another thing that can be done the first day is to introduce the students to the room you will share with them for the year. Show them the furniture and books in the room and tell them of other resources available. Show them the supplies and equipment in the room, open the doors to them. Ask students what they would like to do with what is available. Suggest that they add to the richness of the environment by bringing in things they care about. Talk about what you are interested in doing yourself. There is no need to preach a non-authoritarian sermon and many reasons for not doing it. Students generally distrust all sermons, regardless of their message. An open classroom develops through the actions of the teacher and not because of his words.

An Ordinary Classroom
and Several Not So Ordinary Ones
on the First Day of School
(With a Glimpse of Them
Three Months Later)

Teachers must learn to work in open and creative ways themselves if they want their classrooms to become less authoritarian. Recently I conducted a seminar for teachers which was designed to get the participants to do things rather than to talk about techniques of teaching. For example, instead of discussing the teaching of writing or music or painting, we wrote, made music, and painted.

During one session we all tried to think back to our own earliest experiences in school and to recreate them in writing or through drawing. Most of our memories went back to kindergarten or the first grade, and an unusual number of them were spatial. I remembered my first-grade classroom and how confined and boxlike it felt. The tables were placed in rows and their tops were hard and rectangular. I was afraid that I would move things from their proper places and walked cautiously whenever I left my seat. For the most part I tried to disappear into my chair, hide from the teacher, and let my imagination invest the room with wild and secret places.

Many of the other teachers had similar memories. Some remembered windows they were not allowed to look out of, books and papers that had to be treated reverently, chalk boards with rules and assignments

posted on them, new briefcases that had to be kept neat and clean. The drawings were full of boxes representing rooms, papers, books, tables, buildings —our memories of school were predominantly closed and rectangular.

It is no accident that spatial memories are strong. The placement of objects in space is not arbitrary and rooms represent in physical form the spirit and souls of places and institutions. A teacher's room tells us something about who he is and a great deal about what he is doing.

Often we are not aware of the degree to which the spaces we control give us away, nor conscious of how much we could learn of ourselves by looking at the spaces we live in. It is important for teachers to look at the spatial dimensions of their classrooms, to step back so they may see how the organization of space represents the life lived within it. To illustrate this and give a picture of what differences exist from classroom to classroom I would like to consider some hypothetical classrooms, each with identical furniture and dimensions yet arranged by different teachers. I'll start by examining the spatial organization of these rooms on the first day of school, and then look back at them during the middle of the school year. In this way it may be possible to show the many seemingly minor yet crucial ways in which an open classroom differs from an authoritarian and closed one.

The rooms I have in mind can be found in most schools in the United States. They are rectangular in shape, not too large, and contain chalk boards, bulletin boards, cabinets, windows, and perhaps closets, arranged around the periphery of the rectangle. Occasionally there are a sink and drinking fountain and, in exceptional cases, toilets built into the room. The interior has no partitions and is occupied by combinations of chairs, desks, desk chairs, and tables. The desks are rectangular and the tables rectangular or round. Sometimes the chairs and desks are bolted to the floor but there is a tendency to have movable furniture in newer buildings. The teacher's desk is distinguished from the pupils' desks by its size and the presence of abundant drawer space.[3]

There are some classrooms which also have bookcases, magazine racks, work benches, and easels. Also there are usually wastebaskets in the room.

These are the common elements—now let's turn to the way they are fitted into the classroom environments. The first teacher[4] I want to consider has had several years' experience; she is talented and popular with her pupils. In her room the authoritarian mode of teaching does not seem particularly oppressive. She is an attractive woman and spends time trying to make her room as pleasant as possible. This fits very well with her teaching style. She is quite friendly with her students in a maternal way and prides herself on being able to get them to perform well. She enjoys teaching gifted children the most, but will take her turn with the less bright classes. She is a bit of a cynic yet gets along with the staff. Her main

[3] In colleges teachers are often given lecterns or their desks are placed on platforms or above the level of their students' chairs.

[4] These portraits are fictional versions of classrooms I've visited.

fault (though it is not seen as such by her co-workers) is a deep intolerance of, and dislike for, defiant and "lazy" pupils.

This teacher works very hard getting her classroom in order before the first day of class. She has read the class record cards, knows how many girls and boys there are, who the troublemakers are likely to be. She arranges the desks, tables, and chairs accordingly. The wall with the chalk board is designated the front of the room (many teachers don't realize that this needn't be the case), making the opposite wall the back of the room, and the two remaining walls the sides. This may seem a simple-minded thing to mention but it isn't. Why does a classroom have to have a front, a back, and two sides? The notion that there is a "front of the class" and the authoritarian mode of delivering knowledge received from above to students who are below—both go together.

Having designated the front of the room, the teacher moves all the tables and desks into a position where they face the chalk board. They are also arranged in evenly spaced rows. Chairs are placed accordingly, one to a desk, or to a designated place around a table. Extra chairs and tables are set aside until the teacher's desk is in place. The teacher I'm describing is sympathetic to the progressive movement in education. She doesn't believe that the teacher should put her desk in the front of the room, even though she accepts the notion of a "front" of the room. Consequently she moves her desk to the side, a bit apart from the students' desks but in a convenient position to survey them.

An extra table, round if possible, is placed in the
back of the room. The wastebasket is placed next to
the teacher's desk.

So much for the movable furniture. Next the
teacher turns to the chalk board. On the far right
(or left) of the chalk board in the front of the room
the teacher prints neatly her name (prefaced by
Miss), the class designation, room number, and several other things that may look like this:

> Miss A. Levinton
> Class 6-543 (hs)
> Date
> Attendance: B_____ G_____
> Assignment:
>
> Homework:

After the chalk board come the bulletin boards.
The teacher has prepared ingenious and elegant dis-
plays to put up around the room. There are photo-
graphs, charts, signs, maps—things designed to illustrate and illuminate the curriculum for the year and
make the classroom handsome though somewhat
antiseptic. A small part of one bulletin board is set
aside and neatly labeled "Students' Work."

The bookcase in the back of the room holds the
books the teacher has accumulated, and the table in
the back of the room is labeled "Library Corner."
The cabinets and closets are full of neatly stacked
books and papers, and the teacher checks to see that
their doors are all closed. Another closet, one with
a lock, has been set aside as the teacher's closet. It

has been stocked with a smock, some comfortable shoes, a coffee cup and saucer, and a bottle of instant coffee, etc. It also contains a metal box with the students' record cards.

The classroom is ready to receive its students. The teacher has made the room a familiar place for her to function in and, armed with rules and routines, is ready to face her new class and tell them exactly what will be expected of them in the coming year. The students are free to fit in or be thrown out.

A visitor to the class three months later would be struck by the similarities of the room on the first day and ninety days later. A few changes would be evident, however. There would be neat papers on the bulletin board under the label "Students' Work," as well as a new but equally elegant bulletin board display. There would also be books and papers in the students' desks. But the wastebasket would still be next to the teacher's desk and the library would still be bare except for its label. All would be in order.

It is hard to distinguish between apparent chaos and creative disorder. The next classroom I will describe could present problems for an observer; he would have to attend as much to what is not done as to what is done. Interesting and natural patterns of classroom life can emerge through a collaboration of all the people involved; but this may take time and patience, and one has to have seen the process of development in order to understand the result.

When the second teacher I have in mind arrives before the start of school, the classroom is a mess. The chairs have been piled upon the tables and

pushed into a corner. The teacher, a young man
who has taught for several years, can't make up his
mind what to do with the furniture. As he enters
his room he feels disoriented. He can't tell the front
of the room from the rear. It strikes him that there
may be advantages in seeing the room as a neutral
space without points of orientation. Perhaps his students would also be struck by the neutrality of the
space and see for the first time that many things
could be done with it.

Why not leave the room just as it is and see what
happens when the students enter? He had other
plans, ones carefully nurtured over the summer. He
would set up the tables in small groups and let the
children sit where they chose. He would also turn
the teacher's desk into a resource table which he
would occupy at certain times and which could, he
hoped, become the communications center of the
classroom rather than the seat of power and authority. But the idea of leaving things as they are may
be a better way to begin the year. Perhaps it might
be possible to make organization of the class a
collaborative venture between him and his students,
and among the students themselves. Besides, he
has come to realize that the things that work best
in class for him are the unplanned ones, the ones
that arise spontaneously because of a student's sug-
gestion or a sudden perception. He trusts his intui-
tions and isn't too upset to abandon plans that had
consumed time and energy.

The previous year he had run a reasonably open
classroom. Still he had organized the room from
front to back; and though the tables and chairs were

movable, they faced in only one direction during the
year. He had used the class record cards to tell him
who his pupils were though he very frequently found
them misleading and inaccurate. For half the year
he'd used textbooks and finally got up the courage
to drop them after one of his pupils turned in a
devastating parody of one of the stories in the book.
He had worried that the principal of the school might
object to this but he did not announce what he was
doing and no one complained. During the remainder
of the year he built a library of students' writing and
books to replace the textbooks. He found one interesting set of readers and kept them because he liked
group reading himself and wanted to have one book
he could read together with his students and discuss
with them. That was one of his pleasures in teaching.

He also managed to piece together a set of diction-
aries and obtain a record player and a collection of
records, a slide machine, a $15 tape recorder, tapes
and film strips, and a miscellaneous collection of
junk that filled the closets of the room leaving him
no place to hang his coat. He took to hanging it in
the wardrobe along with his students' coats.

The stuff he had collected the previous year was
still in the closets and cabinets. He threw open all
the doors in the room as he had planned. The blackboard and bulletin boards in the room had been un-
touched since June as he had requested. Except for
the tables and chairs everything was as it was the last
day of school the previous year.

The plan was quite simple. The first day of school
would consist of a dismantling of the previous year's

work, an examination of things in the classroom by the new students, and an exploration of what was available. He didn't want to impose a structure upon the class; at the same time he knew that it was crucial to have enough stuff in his room to suggest to his pupils the range of things they might do.

It is impossible to predict what his classroom would look like after three months. That would depend upon the students and the teacher, and also upon what happened to be engaging their attention at the moment. Things would most certainly be in a state of flux. Certain groupings of chairs and tables would be just forming, others would be in the process of disintegration. The bulletin boards would be full of the students' works, or of pictures they liked or the teacher liked. Some might look worn but sacred and bound to last out the year; others would be in the process of being assembled or dismantled. The stuff—the record player, tape recorder, books, etc.— would be distributed throughout the room and there is no telling where the wastebasket would be. Those who needed it would use it—and would not have to come up to the teacher's desk in order to throw things out.

The teacher's desk might also be anywhere. It might not even be the teacher's any more, the teacher settling for a desk like the pupils' and abandoning his privileged piece of furniture to some other use.

In order to find out what this all meant, an observer would have to discover what the pupils were doing and what the teacher was doing at that particular moment in the year. The observer might not discover chaos, however, but a more complex and freer order than is usually found in classrooms in the United States, or in the society at large for that matter.

It may be useful to look at a third classroom. The room and its furniture are the same but it is in a high school where not one but four or five classes use it daily. It is the teacher's room in a more real sense than is possible in the elementary school since the teacher is the only person there throughout the school day.

There is another problem—the teacher is a specialist. She has been hired to teach a specific subject and, by virtue of that fact, is restricted in her own freedom. Still within limits this teacher has managed to have an open class—or rather, four open classes, since she is required to teach four different English[5] classes a day. The students in her classes are grouped according to what the school considers to be ability, and whatever her personal opinion of tracking, she has to teach tracked classes. She has a

---

[5] English is not the only subject that can be presented in an open classroom. I have seen history, science, math, and physical education classes based on non-authoritarian principles. In each case the teachers introduce the students to the possibilities for learning in their subjects and then step back and let the students discover what they care to learn. A science lab or the equipment room of a gym are wonderful places to explore. In math there are many problems of measurement, timing, bargaining, gambling that can be presented. In history there are central themes such as war, exploitation, love, and power that can be explored. It is surprising how naturally students respond to being presented with choices in any subject.

"bright" class, a "slow" class, and two middle classes. There are several tables and many movable chairs with armrests in the room. There are also many makeshift bookcases filled with dozens of books, magazines, newspapers, collections of students' writing. The walls still have the previous year's accumulation of writing, drawings, cartoons on them. A section of wall is covered with newsprint and set aside for the students' graffiti (a possible form of writing).

The teacher's main problem is to make her room available to all four classes in the same way. There are temptations to simplify things, have a pet class and structure the room for them. The "bright" class is an easy one to choose since the students in it are usually cooperative.[6] The room can be arranged for them and the other three classes that use the room would have to squeeze themselves into a space designed for the bright students.

Another way of dealing with the situation would be to neutralize the room—place the chairs and desks in columns and rows and force each class to sit segregated according to sex, and arranged in alphabetical order.

Yet chairs and tables can be moved about every

---

[6] This may be changing. Bright students in many schools I have visited recently are the leaders of student movements and feel social action is more important than academic success. This poses a great problem for authoritarian administrators since the threat of giving poor grades to rebels no longer holds much force. One administrator complained to me that when he threatened to fail some A-track students they told him to go ahead since they didn't care to succeed in his type of school. He felt disarmed—and he was. His only resort was to call in the police to control his students.

period. It is possible, though a bit noisy, to let the students in each class decide their own placement. The hypothetical teacher I'm describing here has gotten used to noise and accommodated herself to a constantly changing space. She even finds advantages in having her students move the chairs each period. It brings the students together, calms them down, and enables them to experience a return to stability during a day in which they are forced to move from space to space every 45 or 50 minutes.

The first day of school in this classroom is hard to describe. Each class that visits the teacher starts in its own way. The students are forced to move the chairs about and find their own places. Four different arrangements of space exist within that room. The same is true three months later.

I know teachers who can manage four classes and four different arrangements of space a day. Yet few people can live with this institutionalized schizophrenia and no one should be made to function within it. The idea that a teacher can offer something to four or five groups of twenty-five to thirty-five young people each day at intervals of 50 minutes is absurd. Exceptional people can do creative things within the departmental structures as they exist today in high schools and junior high schools—but at what cost to themselves?

Teachers must fight for a sane existence for themselves as well as for their pupils. At the same time they must not turn their frustrations and sense of powerlessness upon their pupils and compound the miseries of school existence. In the sanest circumstances students are allies and not enemies.

During the first year of teaching there are as many problems with the surroundings in which one works as with oneself and with the students. Beginning to teach in a school is like moving into a furnished apartment. One has no familiarity with the furniture, the lighting, the resources, or the drawbacks of the room. For example, it is impossible to estimate beforehand the effect the position of doors and windows in the room will have upon the movement of students and consequently upon the life of the class. I remember my first classroom. It was in an old school and the windows were six feet from the floor. The students couldn't look out into the world and there was a sense of the room being sealed off from the outside. The next year I was in a newer school. My room had a wall of large windows facing on a busy street. The world was practically in the room. I couldn't keep from looking out myself since so much was happening on the street, and so window-watching became one of the activities that were possible in the class.

Doors are often more troublesome than windows. For example, during a school day there is a constant stream of messengers and monitors that enter the room. The farther away the door is from the center of activity the more time monitors and messengers spend in the room, and the more chance they have to distract one's students. On the other hand there is an advantage to the door being away from activity. Nosey teachers and administrators will see less when they sneak a look into the room.

Beginning teachers always worry about mastering school routines—taking attendance, collecting lunch money, appointing monitors, distributing and collecting books and papers, etc. Spatial malaise is as great a problem as all of these and underlies most of them. One doesn't know how to move throughout the room, how to use the light. All of this develops with familiarity and most of it without any conscious awareness of change. The second year is often easier than the first because the setting of one's encounter with young people is familiar and comfortable. One of the most important and helpful things a teacher can do is explore the space of his classroom with and without his pupils and make it as comfortable and familiar a place as possible.

II

Planning and Lesson Plans

In most schoolrooms the use of time is as rigidly planned as the use of space. The usual device for alloting time is the lesson plan. Before discussing planning I think it may be useful to look at examples of two quite different types of lesson plans. The first (page 47) is common in most schools. Publishers produce preruled plan books for teachers, and administrators often require that a plan be entered in one of these books and submitted the first day of the week, before classes meet.

The second lesson plan is more anecdotal. It consists of a teacher's notes to himself on the way things might develop in his classroom; it is also a diary of events in the classroom as the teacher perceives them.

Lesson Plan I

Lesson Plan I	M	T	W	Th	F
Topic	The short story overview—text pp. 6-10	The Retrieved Ref. O. Henry text pp. 13-17	Ret. Reform. O. Henry pp. 18-25	The Dead James Joyce pp. 26-30	The Dead
Sources	Textbook containing intro. on short story and 12 sample stories	Name of textbook	Name of textbook and pocket book of O.H. stories	Name of text	Same
Aims-Objectives	To appreciate the short story as a form of writing and to know the characteristics of the short story	To appreciate O.H.'s contribution to the short story form; to understand his development of character .	To understand notion of transformation in O.H.—to see why Ret. Ref. is good short story; see how it relates to other forms of the short story	To appreciate a different form of short story	More of same—Tie together the two short stories
Methods	Read text, list the forms of the short story and sketch the history of short story from de Maupassant to X	Read ½ of story and talk about following words: 1) retrieved 2) reformation Consider the following questions: 1), 2), 3)		To read aloud	Finish story, then develop following points: 1), 2)
Evaluation	As homework answer questions: 1)-what is main idea of short story? 2) .... 3)		To give test of following form: ─		To write two paragraphs comparing O.H. and Joyce, considering 1), 2)
Follow up	Assign each student choice of 1 of 33 to r___ by X___		To have pupils do biography of O.H. for extra credit and read and report on ___		

Lesson Plan II

Sunday: O. Henry's story, *The Retrieved Reformation*

I liked it as a kid, seems artificial, phony now. Wonder what the kids will think? Perhaps can talk about other O. Henry endings? Or maybe about prisons, or safecracking tools? Or about what being a criminal means—right and wrong seem so simple in the story. The banker's daughter and family seem too good, too positive—aren't they thieves, too? Is O.H. at all ironic? —Don't know, maybe the kids can bring something fresh to the story which seems so tired and empty to me. Ought to read more O.H. and perhaps more stories about fugitives and about transformations—would Kafka make sense here, or maybe— Have to wait and see how things develop.

Does it make sense to talk about "the short story" first, since I can't put it all together myself and have read enough to know the text's summary is worthless? When we all get together I'll start talking about short stories and see what develops.

Monday: The kids were bored with my pieties about O. Henry and wanted to read the story. My cracks about a safecracker fascinated them. They went through the whole story reading aloud. I don't like that way too much but was swept away. While reading, the kids started talking about a lot of things—mostly about what it must feel like to be liberated from prison. Brenda suggested that it probably isn't much different from what she feels at 3:00 in the afternoon. The bell rang somewhere near the end of the story.

Tuesday: The kids raced through the story and were upset by the ending—a few refused to read beyond the point where the heroine was locked in the safe—it was too phony. Most of the hour was taken up in speculation about safes, bank robberies, and boring, phony women. The general consensus was that there must be better ways to write about life than O.H. discovered.

Lesson plans are supposed to spell out what the teacher is going to do in his classroom day to day, week to week, and even month to month. They are designed to make it possible for administrators to say what ought to be happening at a given moment in all the classrooms of their schools. They are also traps for teachers. If they are followed consistently there develops a smooth temporal progression in the class from one topic to another, with little place for side issues, unexpected discoveries, and unplanned conversations. If a story, or a mathematical concept, or a particular scientific problem is provocative and sends students off in many directions, the lesson plan draws them back to the curriculum and the orderly flow of time in the class day. There are a certain number of stories or science experiments the class *must* go through during the school year. Digressions often make teachers feel nervous and guilty. If an hour is taken up discussing a sidepoint the students will not be able to get through what they have to during the school year.

Time in most schools is considered a precious quantity, and teachers are upset when they feel time is wasted. But the conventional notion of "wasted time" is deceptive. In fact time is wasted in school by all sorts of things—taking attendance, lining up, collecting papers, rehearsing rules and routines. It is also often wasted by going through material that bores everyone and is attended to only by pupils who are the most dependent on the teacher. When people talk to each other and find out about each other they are not wasting time nor is it wasted when students explore what is interesting to them, nor even when students, weary of reading, play a bit, or just sit and draw. It is a fiction that students must follow a set number of procedures in a set time in order to learn to read, think, and make decisions, just as it is a fiction that babies learn to walk and talk by following a prescribed pattern.

There is no one way to learn, nor are there specific stories or experiments all young people *must* go through. The notion that learning is orderly and ought to be identical for all pupils is wrong and in many ways pernicious. It leads to the notion of remedial work—i.e., the idea that students who have not followed the temporal sequence set by the teacher have somehow failed and need remedial attention. Remedy for what? A child who has not learned to read does not need remedial work so much as his own way of learning something for the first time. The idea that a student who has not learned to read by the third or fourth grade is a failure and needs remedial help (special care) can often lead him to believe he is a failure and turn him away from ever caring to read.

There is another aspect of time and order in the classroom that may explain why lesson plans and developmental theories of learning fit so comfortably with the needs of teachers and administrators. I have known teachers who slowed down the tempo of their class when they felt their class would get through the required text and go on to a more "advanced" one appropriate to the next grade. They did it, they claimed, out of consideration for teachers of the next grade level who then wouldn't be able to use the textbooks assigned to them. After all, what could the teachers do without textbooks? The orderly movement of bodies through twelve years of elementary and secondary schools would be disrupted, teachers would have to start thinking for themselves and discover each year where their pupils were at. Each school year would then be unique for teacher and student. This would be the opposite of what exists in schools where teaching becomes an automatic and repetitious experience.

The two examples of lesson plans at the beginning of this section differ considerably. The first, the more standard, orders learning, allocates days and hours to stories, spells out questions and responses, and imposes a single direction upon thought and activity in the classroom. It also imposes (at least on paper) an orderly temporal sequence upon the school year.[1]

---

[1] This matter of breaking down the tyranny of the "curriculum" is one of the most difficult problems facing teachers who are trying to develop open classrooms. Even though the texts are senseless and the children restless and bored, teachers still develop feelings of guilt that they are not "teaching" their students what they're supposed to know. Actually, the whole notion of there being an "orderly sequence" to learning is fallacious. Children's learning is *episodic* rather than vertical or linear. One can think of it

One can predict just what will be covered during the year and can usually tell where the class ought to be during any particular month or week. The school year is to be thought of as having a definite beginning, middle, and end.

The second type of lesson plan is quite different. It does not lay out a plan that must be followed, or tell the teacher how much his pupils ought to be doing each day. Rather it is a guide to the options the teacher provides his class and a means of understanding and assessing where his students are and where they seem to be going. Planning in an open classroom is itself a creative activity and involves as much looking back in time as looking forward. It also involves thought and serious study. Of course it is possible for a class to read a story together in an open classroom. But if the teacher is presenting a story to the class, the students should have the right not to read the story, or not to participate in the discussion. The teacher can set themes, ask questions, etc. So can the students. In reading O. Henry's story together with the students the teacher does not present the work as a masterpiece the students must learn to appreciate. It is a work some may like and others might find boring. It is also a work that some students might not even care to finish.

---

as a spider web rather than as a staircase. Happily, more recent studies by psychologists and other experts are beginning to point this out. See especially Kenneth Wann, et al., *Fostering Intellectual Development in Young Children,* Bureau of Publications, Teachers College, 1962, and J. McVicker Hunt, *Intelligence and Experience,* Ronald Press, 1961.

Discussion of the story can move in any number of directions; and the teacher should anticipate as many of these as possible, thinking about things that might interest the students. For *The Retrieved Reformation,* that might mean anticipating the possibility of exploring prisons, safes, locks, the origin of criminal acts, personal change, banks, O. Henry's use of language, etc. The more the teacher is prepared himself to follow what seems to interest his students, the more likely they are in turn to try to draw the teacher out and discover what he knows.

The teacher also ought to think about other options he can present to his students in connection with their reading a story together. They could write their own stories, parody the story they read, act it out, change it, write a sequel, read other O. Henry stories, or, if it seems to be the will of the class, drop the whole thing and go on to something else.

In some schools it is not so easy to move freely into topics the students find relevant. Teachers are often forced by administrators or state requirements to cover specified texts in equally specified time units. I chose the familiar O. Henry story to illustrate the two lesson plans, because the choice of a story to begin with may not be open to teachers. The curriculum may trap them as well as their students into considering work that is mediocre or boring. One strategy that teachers who feel that their jobs depend upon sticking to the curriculum might consider is parody. Silly or irrelevant texts can be rewritten by students, parodied, and turned into something else. They can be considered psychologically and sociologically; for example, the minds and social views of textbook writers themselves can be examined critically. No matter what material is forced upon the class, students can learn much from a teacher who laughs at a silly or stupid text or is angry at a racist one.

To plan intelligently, the teacher must observe the class and assess what is happening: who is interested in what, who isn't, what directions the students are moving in. Only in this way can the teacher discover what the students' interests and abilities may be. As students become interested in different aspects of a subject the teacher can provide them with books, hints, suggestions, references. Planning in a non-authoritarian classroom must be based on the possibility of abrupt changes. Subjects arise and are dropped or develop in many different ways. There is no predicting who will be interested and active at a given time.

There must be a beginning of the school year simply because school starts on a certain day in September. But there should be no "middle" or end, in any formal sense, to the school year. This is not to imply that the teacher and students should not look back on what they have done, try to assess what has happened in the classroom, or gain perspective on what they have learned. Such reconsiderations are valuable and necessary. Yet they ought to occur naturally when people feel they are moving from one phase to another. "Perceiving" what has been done in the class should mean that the class will learn something new about what has been happening.

III

Some Classrooms
in Operation

Teachers often ask me to give them concrete examples of open classrooms in operation. Yet there is a danger in citing examples, for people often use them as models to imitate. There is no single model open classroom. Rather there are as many variations as there are combinations of students and teachers. However, there is value in learning what others have done and so I would like to share several experiences I have had recently in the Berkeley Unified School District that have been helpful to me.

The first experience happened in a first grade class.[1] I have been working with the teacher and student teacher in the class. We planned to try several word games and see how the children responded. I was in the room with the student teacher and about twenty children. The teacher was out talking to the parents of one of the boys in the class.

The room is quite large and has many centers of activity and no one center of authority. It takes a

---

[1] The classes described here are at Oxford Elementary School in Berkeley, and the teachers mentioned are Carol Morel, Susan Risso, and Ted Morgan.

while to discover that the desk in the corner, piled with papers and books, and without a chair next to it, is the teacher's desk. In one corner of the room is a cozy discussion area formed by planks placed on cinder blocks. The children have painted on the planks and sit on them when they have group discussions. Another corner has a club area with cushions on the floor and butcher paper on the walls for the students to write and draw on. There is a table with art supplies along one wall, a table with animal cages in the middle of the room, and another one with finished works of art next to it. The students' tables are clustered in small groups throughout the rest of the room, and students' work hangs on all the walls.

The students in the class were just beginning to get involved in reading, and we wanted to find ways of keeping them interested in the written word without putting them through endless drills in reading workbooks. We wanted to avoid destroying the students' initial motivation to learn how to read. I suggested a game that a group of teachers tested on themselves the week before. The children would make the whole room into a poem by placing cards with words they selected on objects in the room and reading the cards in sequence. Such random poetry can produce interesting juxtapositions of words, objects, and ideas, and be a lot of fun to create.

The student teacher agreed to introduce the idea of the game to the class and see what happened. We would plan what to do next after observing the children's response. For some reason that morning the students were restless. We all sat around on the planks and the student teacher tried to get everyone's attention. He had a blank index card in one hand and tried to explain the idea of making the room into a poem. However, fights and teasing broke out. Few children listened and he was clearly getting angry. After five minutes, during which tension was building, he turned to several boys who were the worst offenders and said, "If you don't want to listen, why don't you do something else?" That rescued the situation. Instead of demanding that the boys listen and provoking a confrontation, he offered them an option which they immediately accepted. They went to the clubhouse corner and played at being lions and tigers that ate teachers. Then he went on describing the game to the rest of the class.

Still the children seemed puzzled and unresponsive. I suggested we go ahead and ask the children to pick words we could write on the blank cards and forget about making explanations. The children immediately responded, choosing words like "butterfly," "teacher," "bossy," "love," "hate." After writing the words on the cards we gave the children some tape and suggested they put them somewhere in the room. Explaining was obviously less effective than doing.

The children eagerly chose their words, but they wouldn't hang them on objects in the room. They preferred to tape the cards on themselves and/or other people. Instead of making the room into a poem they made people into poems. Instead of insisting that the class do as we planned, the student teacher and I decided to follow the children's lead, and made ourselves into poems too.

By this time the boys in the clubhouse joined us—

we were having too good a time and they didn't want to miss it.

After running about for a while with words taped to their bodies, the children formed small groups and read their collective poems. Several boys decided to form a poetry club and record all the class poems, while other children collected all the word cards and stuck them to the blackboard. Then the class put aside words for a while and went out to recess. Our planning for the next time was based on what we had observed during that period.

I have been working with another class in that same school, a kindergarten class. This room is also a complex place. There are several typewriters in one corner, a music center in another, a doll house and furniture in a third. One door in the room exits to the playground while the other leads to the hall. Throughout the room there are other centers—an open space with low chairs to sit around on, tables, a cabinet with a tape recorder, a movable stand with a 16mm projector, bookcases used as dividers creating many small spaces. The teacher and I have tried many things together, but there are two that are particularly interesting.

One day Danny Caracco, one of my colleagues, and I brought a hundred feet of blank film leader to class and showed it to the children. They picked up their magic markers and paints and inks and made a film of colors and shapes. There was no need for instruction. Before we could say a word about how to make a film, the children were already making one. Before we had a chance to talk about the product of their work we were overwhelmed by their desire to see it—and to make a sound track to it, and to dance to their sound track, and to play the film on their bodies while they were dancing, and to flick the lights in the classroom on and off while all this was happening. In a few hours these kindergarten children had developed their own "mixed media" technology. We had just stepped aside and let them learn and teach us.

The other experience with the kindergarten class is harder to describe. I teach a class at Berkeley High School, which is euphemistically titled Children's Theater. There are twenty young people in the class and we do improvisations, events in supermarkets, buses, anywhere in the community at large. The class meets formally in the costume room of the Berkeley Community Theater, though our classroom is the city we live in. I have found myself increasingly unable to accept the four walls of a schoolroom as the boundaries in which learning is supposed to take place. Our class goes where we feel we can learn and may be able to teach. We have had picnics on weekends, done improvisations on the beach, in parks, on the streets, in the supermarket. We have also talked about the irrelevance of school and the need to work, to become a functioning part of the community while young and full of the energy needed to change institutions. Doing theater in public places is one thing. Another and more important one is infiltrating the institutions that control lives—hospitals, banks, gas stations, supermarkets—and humanizing them. School at its best can be a place where young people can come to know themselves, their strengths and weaknesses, and get themselves ready to change a society which makes so little sense.

The classroom not only segregates young people from society. It segregates them from each other. We have elementary schools, junior high schools, high schools—six-year-olds never meet ten- or fifteen- or seventeen-year-olds in school. It is absurd. Not only do we not let children of the same age teach each other by insisting upon silence in the classroom, we make it impossible in the context of school for older children[2] to teach younger ones. Our "Children's Theater" class has moved away from this, and once a week we visit a kindergarten.

The first time ten high school students came to the kindergarten we were all anxious about the visit. No one knew what would happen. A few improvisations were tried and they were fun but something unexpected and perfectly natural happened. The kindergarten children wanted to know who the high school students were, what they did and cared about. They wanted a chance to find people they liked, or whose interests fascinated them. The high school students felt the same way. The teacher and I, adults and the presumed experts in the room, stepped aside and let things happen.

Groups formed and dissolved, a few people went outside to take a walk, one high school student started to explain drawing to the young children and attracted a crowd, another began to use a type-

---

[2] I feel uneasy about this word. It makes some sense when applied to kindergarten or first grade people but none whatever when applied to high school students.

writer, and got another crowd. I don't know everything that happened that morning, because so much
was going on at the same time. What was clear was
that the rich classroom we had functioned in with the
kindergarten class was poor and meager compared to
what it became with many young people alive and
"unsupervised" in it.

Most of my examples are drawn from English and
art classes. That is not because they are the only or
easiest subjects in which to develop open environments. The reason I use these examples is that I
know them best. Recently I have seen a science class
at the Berkeley Community High School that em-
bodies the same principles.

John Rosenbaum is a physicist and an artist. He
makes light boxes using polarized lights and filters. It
is difficult to walk into his classroom and not be
drawn into an exploration of the phenomena of light
and sound. There are sounding boards, tuning forks,
musical instruments, amplifying equipment, etc., in
one part of the room. Another part has strobe lights,
polarized lights, filters, colored gels. And there are
science books about, too. And art books. It is a
magical world where one can start by playing with
color and sound, and become involved in studying
those phenomena in artistic or scientific ways.

There is another aspect of John's room which I
must mention. In a corner is a large closet. It is
empty except for rugs on the floor and posters on the
walls. It is a meditation room for students (and
hopefully for faculty as well), a place to go alone
and be alone. It is the only place available for con-
templation in Berkeley High School, which has al-

most 3,000 students, and it is considered strange. It is legitimate for a kindergarten or first grade classroom to have a clubhouse or private place for young people, but we never think older children need to be alone in classrooms.

Science and art are considered opposites in school and by thinking it teachers make it so. Recently the opposite of this happened with a group of students I was working with. We started out by telling a collective story—one line each. As the story evolved the main characters would find themselves in difficult positions and would escape by transforming themselves into animals. I followed the theme of transformation by suggesting that we all transform ourselves into anything we wanted, and write a description from the point of view of the creature we became. The students became cats, flies, caterpillars, in one case a boiling potato, and in another a withering Aztec god. I became a left hand.

After writing we drew pictures of the world through the eyes of our creature selves and then did an improvisation. We became physically the creatures we were transformed into. We then had to create some relationship with each other. One of the girls in considering that problem in improvisation asked me if a boiling potato could worship a withering Aztec god.

From the transformation of ourselves we began to talk about magical transformation, and about the transformation of physical objects. This naturally led to alchemy and from there to chemistry. This whole experience led me to understand chemistry in a new and exciting way and to restore some of the magic of chemical change that had been lost for me in school through tediously having to memorize formulas and facts.

Not long ago I was looking through a series of science curriculum guides produced by the Science Curriculum Improvement Study.[3] These guides are based on discovery principles, i.e., on the notion that the student learns best when he discovers things for himself rather than by being told them or from reading them in a book. They provide a first step away from textbooks, though in my mind they do not go far enough since they determine what it is a student ought to discover. However they are well done and worth looking at. My point in mentioning them here is that it struck me how limited they were by confining themselves to the sciences. I would like to take some of the specific units and speculate upon how they can involve more than what is narrowly construed as science. The ones I will consider here are entitled: *Interactions, Relativity, Systems and Subsystems,* and *Environments.*

1. *Interactions* can be looked upon as a study of the relationships between physical objects. It can also be looked upon as a study of the relationship between individuals (psychology), groups (sociology), nations (history), ideas (?). Interactions can be danced out, developed in improvisational drama, or studied in literature or the mass media. Interac-

---

[3] Further information can be obtained from Professor Robert Karplus, Lawrence Hall of Science, Berkeley, California.

tions in the scientific sense can be looked at as a subclass of all the systems of interactions that man is involved in.

2. *Relativity* need not be confined to relativity physics. One can study moral principles and values, examine the relativity of cultures, listen to alternate musical systems (8 tone, 5 tone, 12 tone), even create musical instruments and systems that have their value relative to other musical systems. One can also study relatives (I'm his cousin, he's my cousin, but I'm his uncle and he's my nephew) and then kinship systems. One can also talk about looking at the world through other eyes and trying to understand the experience of other people and creatures. One can dance out the movement of two independent systems moving with relationship to each other.

3. *Systems and Subsystems.* Think of a jazz combo as a system with several subsystems, one, for example, the rhythm section and another (within the rhythm section) the subsystem of drums and cymbals. Listen to the musical group as a whole and then listen to the subsystems. Or, again, take a game like football—think of the whole team, the offense, the defense, the linemen, the quarterback, the running backs. Play the game and look at films of the game the way you would look at a physical system to be studied in physics. Then look at the game as a dance. Move from one mode of perception and thought to another. The free play of imagination and intellect is certainly one of the components of creative thought in any discipline.

4. *Environments.* One can study physical environ-

ment. One can also create environments. Recently I
worked with a group of youngsters who created a
suburb out of cardboard tubes, string, and paper.
As we developed the suburb we became the residents
of our environment and acted out the lives of people
we created. Using the simplest and cheapest materials
one can recreate the world in the classroom. One
can look at contemporary art, at the environments
of Andy Keinholtz, Claes Oldenburg, Allan Kaprow,
or study theater as a means of creating a simulated
environment. One can look at the magic of storytell-
ing and fiction where at their best convincing worlds
are spun out of words.

IV
Ten Minutes a Day

People who have been students in authoritarian classrooms cannot expect themselves to develop their own open classrooms easily. I started out as an authoritarian teacher. It was the only way I knew to teach; the way I had been taught. It took several years before I was able to function in a freer environment. Indeed, the students were much more ready for freedom than their teacher was. Perhaps it was better to start tentatively than to pretend that a change had come over me suddenly, and to try to turn everything upside down in the classroom. My beliefs in a free, non-authoritarian classroom always ran ahead of my personal ability to teach in one.

There are several ways to experiment in the classroom. It depends upon who the teacher is. One ought not to try something basically incompatible with one's personality. It is likely to cause frustration and hostility, and to make further experimentation seem more dangerous than it really is. A crucial thing to realize is that changing the nature of life in the classroom is no less difficult than changing one's own personality, and every bit as dangerous and time-consuming. It is also as rewarding.

The starting point of change is discontent. If you are perfectly content with an authoritarian style of teaching and pleased with your pupil's lives in the classroom there, an attempt to change will be pointless. Some of the best authoritarian teachers, often charming and brilliant people who succeed in persuading young people to perform what the school demands and to like it at the same time, may find change irrelevant.

If, on the other hand, the authoritarian mode is distressing—if being an unquestioned authority is too difficult and unpleasant a role to sustain, if the boredom of your pupils or the irrelevance of what they are learning distresses you, then perhaps other approaches should be tried. Before doing so you should try to think as honestly as you can about your teaching experience and try to articulate to yourself or a friend what it is that makes you want to change. It also may be of use to remember yourself as a pupil in school—to think back to your early experiences of frustration, joy, anxiety, learning, boredom in the classroom. I found that my memories of school helped me to avoid doing hateful things to my pupils that my teachers had done to me. This isn't to say that you will be able to make a list of all that's troubling you. But it is a good way to begin perceiving the classroom as a place where strong and interesting experiences take place, rather than one where the objective performances of students are measured.

One way to begin a change is to devote ten minutes a day to doing something different. There is never any problem of finding ten minutes to play with, since what the pupils "must cover" is usually padded in order to fill up time. During that ten minutes present the class with a number of things they can choose to do. Present them with options you feel may interest them. Allow them the option of sitting and doing nothing if they choose. Moreover, make it clear that nothing done during that period will be graded, and nothing need be shown or explained to the teacher. That ten minutes is to be their time and is to be respected as such. Step out of the way and observe the things your pupils choose to do.

Step out of the way, but don't disappear. Make it clear that you won't tell people what to do or how to do it, but that you will be available to help in any way you can, or just to talk. For ten minutes cease to be a teacher and be an adult with young people, a resource available if needed, and possibly a friend, but not a director, a judge, or an executioner. Also try to make it possible for the ten minutes to grow to fifteen, twenty, so long as it makes sense to you and your pupils. It is not unlikely that those ten minutes may become the most important part of the day, and after a while may even become the school day.

Some specific hints on the use of the ten minutes:

—in English class it is possible to read, write (set three or four themes and leave it open for students to develop other ones), talk, act.
—in mathematics the students can set problems, solve problems, build computers, compute, design buildings (or other structures or things), talk about money, set problems for each other and the teacher.
—in social studies it is possible to talk about his-

tory; about newspapers, events, people; write
about them; compose or listen to poems, play
songs about them; talk or invite people in to
talk about what's happening.

—in all classes students can do nothing, gossip,
write, start a newspaper, a newsletter, listen to
music, dance, talk about or play games, bring
in things that may interest the teacher or other
students and talk about them, write about
them. . . .

Think about what is happening during those ten
minutes and learn to be led by the students. If certain things are particularly interesting to one group,
find out about those things, learn as much as you
can, and, seeing their interest, present them with
ways of getting more deeply into what they care
about. If, for example, a group of students is interested in animals and their relationship to people, you
can refer them to fables, to Konrad Lorenz, to experimental psychology, to whatever you can discover
yourself. And if you don't know about such matters
find someone who does, and invite him to class to
meet your pupils.[1] Then—and this is crucial—step
out of the way again. Do not insist that because
you have uncovered all these new options for your
students that they *must* pursue them. Maintain your
own freedom from the authoritarian mode and help

---

[1] It is always a good idea to bring as many non-teachers
into your classroom as possible. Painters, writers, businessmen, journalists all have valuable experience to offer young
people that teachers don't have. So do people who have no
specific vocations to talk about.

your students maintain their freedom, however modest it may be. Learn, though it is difficult, to allow your students to say "No" to what you want them to learn no matter how much stake you have in it. This means that one must understand one's own stake in making young people learn what one wants them to learn and not take it overseriously. Teachers must develop a sense of what they look like to young people and understand how pointless and even funny it can seem to young people to see adults losing their cool over someone's refusal to take the division of fractions or the imagery in Act I of Macbeth seriously.

Opening Out

In public schools learning is supposed to take place within the classroom. Occasionally a class takes a supervised trip to a museum, a library, or a ball game. These experiences, however, are considered secondary to "real" learning, which consists of reading books, looking at educational material (films, models of machines, etc.), and listening to the teacher. I remember taking my sixth grade class out of school two days a week. We walked around the community, visited factories, the university, artists' studios, chemical laboratories, film studios, people's houses, supermarkets, furniture stores, etc. Many other teachers at the school felt that our trips were not educational, and that we were leaving school so that I could avoid doing "real" teaching and the students could avoid submitting to "real" learning.

But the trips were a vital part of our experience together. We saw some of the world, talked to people, got a sense of the environments in which different types of work are done, and in a few places made friends and set up after-school programs for the students. The kids got a sense of what adults do with their time and a feel for possible careers for themselves.

Not everything we saw was pleasant. We went to court, the welfare department, the police department, the children's shelter. We hung around and watched and recorded the ways that our society deals with people. And when we returned to class we had things to talk about and study in depth. We compared, for example, our impressions of factory work with the one presented in the school's vocational guidance manual. We talked of justice as we saw it work against poor and black people in the courts and as the civics textbook explained it.

Visits are valuable, but they are limited. First impressions are often misleading. I feel that it would be a very good thing if young people could spend time as apprentices to artists, technicians, businessmen, etc. They could also be participant observers in places of work, and plan some of their program in the classroom around their experiences away from the school. This year some of my students will spend time at a TV studio, a design workshop, a boutique, a highway construction job, a laboratory, and at several departments of the University of California.

Schools are afraid to let their students go into the world away from the critical eye of the teacher. It won't be easy to leave the school several times a week with the class, much less develop apprenticeships for individual students away from the school building. However, you can move slowly, and should get as much help from the kids' parents as possible. Visit where they work, get to know the neighborhood you teach in. Ask the kids to tell you what's happening and to take you places. If there are places they feel you shouldn't know about, don't press.

The whole community ought to be the school, and the classroom a home base for the teachers and kids, a place where they can talk and rest and learn together, but not the sole place of learning. The classroom ought to be a communal center, a comfortable environment in which plans can be made and experiences assessed. However one can open up the classroom as much by moving out of it as by changing the life within it.

Note: Increasingly, people are abandoning the public schools as hopeless. They have been setting up schools in storefronts, parks, homes, and factories. These schools use the community much more than do the public schools. There are many people around who care about the young and are delighted to give their time and energy. They are not "professional" teachers and therefore would have a difficult time finding places in public schools. They do things like make films, or paint or write poems, or build houses and highways, design and manufacture machines, deal with human relations or with marketing products. Often they will be delighted to come into the classroom and will invite kids to visit them at their work.

It is important for teachers to seek out people who do things and bring them into the classroom. It's not so hard—often all that is necessary is to go to a place, announce that one is a teacher, and invite people to come to class and meet the kids. There are, however, school administrators who will resist visitors they can't completely control. In these cases it may make sense to invite people anyway and not tell anybody. The more adults the kids get to know, the more easily they can move in a world which is still, after all, largely controlled by adults.

V

Discipline

As matters stand in schools now, students have no rights. They must do as they are told or they are considered "discipline problems." If they are not interested in learning what the teacher insists they learn they are said to "lack motivation." The problems of motivation and discipline are intricately involved with the authoritarian role of the teacher.

If the teacher considers defiance, disagreement, fights, or refusal to do a particular piece of work, to keep silent, or to line up, as a threat to authority, then a "problem" is created. If, on the other hand, these are considered incidents naturally occurring in the course of communal life, to be adjudicated and absorbed into the whole, they need not be seen as problems.

Punishment is a dangerous way to deal with behavior. If two individuals are punished for fighting, the causes of the fight will not have been resolved. To their hostility toward each other a new hostility toward the teacher and his authority will develop. This doesn't mean that the teacher should stand back from fights and let his pupils tear each other apart. Certainly he should break up the fight. But it is the next step that is crucial. The teacher can punish the fighters, give them bad conduct marks, send them to the principal; or he can do something entirely different. He can turn to them and say, "What's the matter?" and talk about it, wait until calm has returned to the class, and let things proceed. Or he can take the participants aside together, or one at a time. The point is that the event be treated as an affair in the lives of men, and not as a breach of discipline.

Of course this doesn't mean that every time there is a fight the teacher must put aside everything else and explore the issues. Sometimes it is just as effective to stop the fighting, give the participants a chance to cool down, and continue with reading or whatever else the class is doing at the time. There are even times when the fight should be left to end naturally. One must use one's intuition in dealing with conflict.

A good habit for teachers to develop is to begin to ask "Why?" of all the rules and breaches of discipline that occur in the classroom. Why must students never call out? Why must they line up in the same way every day? Why mustn't they talk to each other? Why must they line up, raise hands, do homework?

It is not easy for the teacher to give up his power to punish and to enforce, whether through grades, referrals, or physical punishment. Yet if an open classroom is to develop, the teacher has to learn to abdicate some of the power the school confers upon him. He has to be able to say I'm not going to grade, or I'm not going to punish people, or I'm not going to send anybody to the principal—and mean it. This isn't easy. To announce such principles to one's class and go back upon them is to institute confusion and ask for trouble. Perhaps it is best to begin slowly and with qualifications—I'm not going to grade unless I'm forced to, or I'm not going to send anyone to the principal except in an emergency.

Absolute statements, even on the side of freedom, are dangerous because in the course of human affairs exceptions are bound to arise. I think of a rule I once declared too absolutely. Whenever a knife came out of anyone's pocket for whatever reason, it was to be confiscated. One day a knife fell out of the pocket of one of my pupils while we were playing basketball. The class looked at me to see what I would do, and I followed my rule, as the student stormed off in a rage. A real "problem" could have developed if he hadn't been able to get another knife by the next day. There was no way I could have maintained the rule, maintained face with the rest of the class, and done the humane thing with my pupil. I was trapped by my own rule. That wasn't the only time and I had to teach myself to abandon absolute pronouncements.

In forgoing his power to administer discipline, the teacher must realize that words alone won't convince the students that things are going to be different in his class. The teacher's actions over a period of time reveal to the students whether the teacher means what he says. Because of this, the first year, during which a teacher tries to integrate conflict into the classroom rather than suppress it, can be extremely difficult. The teacher is often uncertain, presenting himself as free and relaxed one day, stern and authoritarian the next. In moments of crisis quite understandably he might fall back on authoritarian attitudes.

The movement to an open classroom is a difficult journey for most of us. The easiest way to undergo it is to share it with one's pupils—to tell them where you hope to be and give them a sense of the difficulty of changing one's styles and habits. Facing uncertainty in oneself, and articulating it to one's pupils, is one way of preventing a superficial bias "against authority" which, if it fails, can lead one to believe that the open classroom just doesn't work. Freedom can be threatening to students at first. Most of them are so used to doing what they are told in school that it takes quite a while for them to discover their own interests. Besides that, their whole school careers have taught them not to trust teachers, so they will naturally believe that the teacher who offers freedom isn't serious. They will have to test the limits of the teacher's offer, see how free they are to refuse to work, move out of the classroom, try the teacher's nerves and patience. All of this testing must be gone through if authoritarian attitudes are to be unlearned.

It is not easy for the teacher either. Freedom in the classroom means freedom for the teacher as well as the students, so the teacher is groping as much as his students. When students are defiant or nasty or disorderly, the teacher naturally will get angry or frustrated. A permissive philosophy would have the teacher accept everything and wait for students to act out their hostilities and confusion. I am not advocating that at all. Rather, I feel a teacher has as much right to be angry, frustrated, impatient, distrustful as the students have and should let them know that. If you are angry with a student for fighting or for refusing to do what you want him to do, tell him and try to deal with the question of why you are angry. If someone tears up a book of yours, express your feelings about it to the students. Only when a teacher emerges as another person in the classroom can a free environment based upon respect and trust evolve. Moreover, if the teacher remains a silent, abused witness to student authoritarianism, a time will come when the teacher has had enough and will take back the freedom he offered the students.

A free way of existing is not necessarily an easy way of existing. Autonomy, the ability to make one's own decisions, and self-direction, the ability to act on one's decisions, can be quite painful to people who have grown up in an authoritarian system.

Troubles and Confrontations

A completely free classroom is not possible within an authoritarian school and an authoritarian school system. At the very least students are required to attend class and this introduces an element of compulsion into even the most open school situation.

A teacher can develop a classroom as open as is consistent with his survival in a given school. The range of a teacher's freedom varies considerably from school to school, and one must assess how much can be gotten away with when looking for a teaching position. Sometimes the more disorganized and demoralized a school, the more one can get away with. An indifferent authoritarian principal can be easier to work with than a "liberal" one who's always looking over your shoulder. Administrators who support open teaching are rare, yet they do exist and it is always worthwhile to look around before you accept a job. It is also important not to base one's impression of a school upon a principal's description of it. Visit classrooms, look at the students' faces, listen to the conversations in teachers' cafeterias, look at the arrangements of space in classrooms, go to lineup and dismissal. Get a sense of the ambiance of the school. One must be wary of apparently liberal administrators who may, in fact, be vicious and vindictive, while giving the impression they are open and accepting people. The best administrator is one who will support you if trouble develops, and liberals are notorious for panicking under pressure.

A non-authoritarian public school is rare, and an authoritarian school with much tolerance for non-authoritarian teaching may be rarer. An open classroom is a threat in a school where the maintenance of control is a central concern. It is a threat to teachers who may find their pupils demanding rights and freedom not acceptable in their classes. It is a threat to supervisors who have a stake in carefully ordered

curricula or who feel the need to know what the
teachers and pupils in their school are doing at every
moment. It is a threat to parents who are fearful for
their children's future and are anxious about their
final grades and test results. It is also a threat, at
first, to students who have been in school too long
and are frightened by freedom. Initially, teaching in
an open classroom can be a lonesome, difficult experience, and the teacher has to be strong and believe it is worth it to himself and to his students.

Survival is always an issue for an innovator and
it is no different for the radical teacher than for any
other revolutionary. Compromises will have to be
made with other teachers, administrators, with one's
own principles, in order to survive, and it will always
be problematic whether they are worth it. Survival
in a given school is not always desirable or possible.
There are times to quit or to be fired, to oppose,
defy, and confront people. This section will be de-
voted to some ways of dealing with an authoritarian
system.

Troubles with Other Teachers

1. *Noise.* An open classroom with many activities
going on simultaneously is not a silent place. Students talk to each other. They also talk to the teacher
and move around from group to group. The noise
in the classroom is not harsh or hysterical, but it

oftens fills the room and can upset other teachers who insist upon silence in their rooms. I have seen teachers become irrationally upset by a noisy classroom, even when they are convinced that the noise was productive and not chaotic. Perhaps noise suggests lack of control and thus activates the authoritarian's fear of his not being in command.

Noise can be modulated but not eliminated. If other teachers are upset you can mention that to the class and together you can decide how to control the volume. If a particular teacher becomes threatening and your supervisors also disapprove of noise then you may be able to find a way to calm the teacher down and negotiate a truce. Perhaps you can find that teacher's weakness and complain about it, instead of being defensive about the noise in one's own room. But the students' right to talk to one another cannot be withdrawn without destroying the openness of your classroom.

2. *Dirt*. Dirt upsets many teachers as much as noise. Everything must be clean and antiseptic as well as quiet in their classrooms. The students can't mess around, they can't decorate the walls without supervision, or drop things on the floor without being corrected. The teacher fears loss of control of the physical environment and in order to maintain power sterilizes it.

An open classroom should not be filthy but it is often messy because many things are happening in it. Students can experiment with things and leave unfinished experiments about the room. They can decorate the walls, use the library, move the furniture about, and generally live comfortably in the room.

Many teachers cannot stand the apparent disorder of an open classroom, but the problem is not so serious as it is with noise. They needn't see disorder if it upsets them. Often it is useful to place a drawing over the window looking into one's room and invite only sympathetic teachers to visit your class. So long as the freedom of your class doesn't spill out of your room many authoritarian teachers will let you go your own way. This is a melancholy fact, and one that some people can't put up with. The degree to which one pretends or refuses to conform is a matter for each teacher's conscience.

3. *Students as Threats*. The students in an open classroom can become threats to other teachers. As information spreads through the student underground that interesting things are happening in your room, you may find curious students passing by and looking in. Welcome them and tell them what is going on. Invite them to poke around and speak to your students. There is no better way to spread the idea throughout the school that there is a different way of teaching. Encourage your students to tell their friends what they are doing, to be living examples of the fact that young people can be people and not merely disenfranchised "children" within the setting of a school. And remember when you receive the hostile stares of teachers you've never met before that your pupils have become "bad examples" for the rest of the school.

There is no direct way I know of to deal with

this hostility, but it is important not to be surprised
by it. Many people in a school do not speak honestly
to others. They bear grudges, spread rumors, are
capable of much pettiness. If at a moment of confrontation many enemies emerge, do not be surprised
or disarmed. Though it may never be explicit, it is
covertly acknowledged in schools that any teachers
and students who manage to get away with free and
open behavior are threats to the survival of the educational system as it now exists.

An Aside on Finding an Ally
and Building a
School Within a School

If possible, find someone in your school with
whom you can talk honestly. It is important to know
someone who will not respond in a hostile or con-
descending way when you talk about your problems or your perceptions of other teachers' problems.
A sign that a teacher is a potential ally is that he is
able to admit his own failures. Still, the admission of
failure can be a liberal ruse to get a new teacher to
talk about himself. One must be intuitive as well as
rational in the choice of allies.

If you are a new teacher it is important to have
an ally who can introduce you to the dangers of your
school. It helps to know whom not to trust. On the
other hand it is also useful to keep oneself open
enough to be surprised. At times the most externally
rigid and cynical teachers turn out to be the most

open and free with their students while the liberal
and progressive ones are covertly hostile and authoritarian.

If you have managed to survive in a school for a
while and have found some friends it is possible to
begin to introduce change on a larger scale. Form a
school within your school with your friends. Schedule
your classes together, share your rooms, let students
move freely from one room to another. Share your
equipment and your individual talents. It doesn't
require any more money or space to reorganize the
school day. One needn't write a proposal or even
ask permission (though sometimes it may make
sense to tell administrators what will be happening).
It may seem a tautology but the way to change
things is by changing them.

I have been working with groups of teachers in the
Berkeley Unified School District, four in one junior
high school, eight in one elementary school, six in
another, and two in a third. Together we are planning ways of creating open subschools within existing
schools. There has been some resistance, but it is
not so powerful or bold as it is when only one teacher
is trying to do something new. My sense is that even
the most conservative administrators and parents
know that something is wrong in the schools. They
can use isolated radical teachers as scapegoats, but
groups of radical teachers frighten them, and they
keep away.

It is possible to get volunteer help for core schools.
Go to local colleges and teacher training institutions,
or to the American Friends Service Committee, or
to the Resistance. Speak to local anti-poverty groups

or community organizing centers. There are many people ready and willing to help in the schools if only they are asked.

To get supplies and equipment go to all the factories in your area and ask for their junk. One can get quantities of used fabric, metal, wood, and plastic free. One can obtain rejects from printing plants and editing scraps from film studios. A whole school program can be supported by the waste produced by our society.

Of course if you don't have friends and can't develop a school within your school, it is still possible to accumulate junk and turn your classroom into the richest and most interesting place in your school.

VI

Troubles with Principals, Assistant Principals, and Other Supervisors

Supervisors deal with teachers in the same way they expect teachers to deal with students. They are usually more interested in avoiding problems and maintaining control than in matters having to do with teaching. As far as they are concerned the content of the curriculum has been mandated by a Board of Education or a curriculum committee, and it is the teacher's role to follow the curriculum. A good teacher, like a good soldier, is one who obeys orders. An excellent teacher is one who obeys them cheerfully and willingly.

I taught at a school with a liberal principal. He ran warm and open faculty meetings and from listening to his rhetoric one would have imagined he actually cared what happened within the classrooms of his school. Yet once he asked the staff to criticize freely the reading program in the school and I did. Perhaps I was being petulant and defiant of authority. I'm not sure. It was my first teaching assignment and I was having a difficult time with my class and often became aggressive. However, the questions I asked were sensible and relevant. They received no answers—only a cold silence and then the meeting passed on to the next item on the agenda.

The teacher sitting next to me said I blew my job at the school, and this was true. At the end of the year I found myself involuntarily transferred to a "bad" school, and it was made clear to me that this was done because I asked too many questions and refused to go along with the principal and the staff and pretend that all was well within the school. It is hard to believe that such small acts of defiance can lead to such drastic action—yet they do, especially where beginning teachers are concerned. You can get away with a lot more if you have been in a school for a few years and have established yourself in the local community of teachers and supervisors. Supervisors are generally eager to get rid of young teachers who are potential sources of bad publicity.

Possibly the most important thing to remember is that supervisors who allow teachers to experiment, and support them, are rare; few are interested in helping teachers cope with problems that arise in the classroom. They judge teachers primarily according to how they fit into the social structure of the school. It is important for young teachers to realize this and not be surprised if their inability to get along with a colleague who has tenure is weighed more heavily against them than success in the classroom is weighed for them. There is little that can be done about this short of changing the people and the structure of the school. That is certainly one long-term objective of developing open classrooms in public school situations. However, the question of survival must be dealt with before the question of victory ever arises. In this respect, there are many different things one might have to do, such as:

—keep two sets of lesson plans, one for the supervisor that follows the curriculum and another for oneself that deals with the reality of one's classroom
—create a set of authoritarian lessons to use when supervisors observe
—be polite and silent at faculty meetings
—seem to comply with administrative directives

There are problems with making hypocritical concessions in order to survive. That is what all teachers do anyway, and unless one makes the concessions in the service of change and is willing on occasion to confront people, the openness of one's classroom will be a lie. It is possible to become another scared teacher talking to students about their freedom and autonomy yet afraid to fight for one's own.

Confrontations

Some confrontations, of course, are unnecessary. It doesn't pay to let every teacher on the staff know what you think of his teaching style and personality the first month of school. Working with young people demands intense concentration and energy which can easily be dissipated in futile fights with foolish teachers.

Confrontations in the teachers' lunchroom are often petty and futile. Teachers say hostile things over lunch and are nervous and distracted by the barbarous custom which allows them no more than forty minutes to swallow their food and rest from their classes. They are particularly hostile toward their students, and they manage to express their frustrations and strains in trying to maintain control of their students. Many of them are not suited to the authoritarian roles expected of them, and yet are afraid to try other ways of teaching. They resent the school, their pupils, and their own lives, especially that part of it which makes it necessary for them to teach. However, their problems cannot be worked out in the teachers' lunchrooms. I found the best thing to do is have lunch in my own room with a few friends. Teachers' lunchrooms are unpleasant places, but no one is compelled to eat in them and it is important to eat in a sane and peaceful place. Also the lunch hour can provide a teacher with a good time to meet his students as individuals.

Yet there are some confrontations that are difficult to avoid and still maintain one's pride. When teachers beat or brutalize students or when they humiliate or insult them, it is difficult not to rush to support the students. Still, school ethics say that a teacher never contradicts or opposes another teacher in front of a child or parent. That rule is perhaps the prime one that governs the social system teachers have evolved in order to live together without destroying each other. The survival of the school is considered more important than the survival of the students, and so it is of secondary importance if the rule leads to the destruction of the students.

Principals who often sympathize with the anger of a young teacher towards the brutalization of students will advise that the teacher wait until the student leaves and then approach the offending teacher rationally. This is nonsense; it is also collusion. I remember a teacher in one of the schools that I taught in. She kicked and smacked and insulted the children and I wanted to do the same to her or at least remove her from the school. She had job tenure, and I had none. I remained silent for a while and my pupils confronted my passive attitude: Why do you let her do it? Are you chicken? Does your job really mean that much to you?

That last is the real question—at what point does your job mean more than being honest and unable to go along with an oppressive system? Everyone must answer that question himself, and, moreover, every teacher must realize that there is no way to avoid facing the question of how much oppression and brutality one can put up with. A refusal to face the question at all is itself an answer.

If you decide to provoke a confrontation with other teachers or with a school administration, I think it is best to gather support and make a public issue out of the confrontation. It is possible to express your feelings, quit, and leave the school as it is. It is also possible to provoke an administration into firing you, and then refuse to leave without a hearing, a public airing of the issues that you feel are the real ones. Recently a teacher was given a letter of dismissal in an Oakland junior high school. The charges against her were refusal to cooperate with the administration. Actually, she insisted that her class receive the books and supplies they were entitled to, and that her students not be suspended from school without a hearing.

She didn't accept the letter and leave politely as the administration expected. Instead she wrote out a list of charges against the principal and presented them to him, to the teachers' union, to the American Civil Liberties Union, to the other teachers in the school, and to her pupils and their parents. Then she demanded a public hearing. At that point the principal told the teacher that he would withdraw his charges if she would withdraw hers. She did, and is still at the school. So is the principal, though his power is not as secure as it had been before the incident.

Another teacher in Richmond was dismissed for being too much involved with his students. He was accused of not following the curriculum, seeing his students after school, telling them about staff conflicts (this was called "unprofessional behavior"), and supporting them in conflicts with certain teachers. He left the system but not before telling his students the entire story, putting all of the documents in their hands, and making it clear to them that just because he was no longer a teacher in their school didn't mean he was no longer their teacher. He still sees them and is trying to help them to change the school.

Teachers must stand with their students and fight for their beliefs and not accept the system's verdict of who is acceptable and who is dangerous and therefore must leave quietly and without a fuss. A teacher can find himself in the midst of political struggles in which he cannot remain neutral. In many ghetto communities parents are determined to take control of the schools and purge racist and incompetent teachers. In other communities reactionary parents are equally determined to purge the school of liberal and non-authoritarian teachers. A teacher who is trying to be bold and creative may find himself in one case allied with parents against the majority of other teachers and administrators, and in the other case find few allies apart from the students. In either case there will be no neutral position for the teacher and therefore he ought to be prepared for political confrontation.

The position of a teacher can be difficult. In some ghetto communities parents may want a rigid authoritarian education for their children so that a teacher who wants to create an open classroom may find himself at odds with people he politically agrees with. There is no general way out of such a dilemma. I suppose the best he can do is explain his work as fully as possible to the parents and ask them to speak to their children about what goes on in his classroom. Also he should show people his students' work. If people are still not convinced, there may be times a teacher has to leave a school voluntarily because political control may be at that point more crucial than non-authoritarian teaching.

One further note: keep a diary that documents your experiences. The document will be invaluable in assessing your own work, and in case of crisis will be your strongest weapon.

VII
Problems

On Becoming Indispensable

There is a way a teacher can experiment with non-authoritarian teaching and be free of other teachers and supervisors. That way is to work with problem students—those students the school system has given up on. Disturbed and retarded and disruptive and delinquent students are in a special category. They are often considered "troubled" simply because they refuse to conform to the authoritarian structure of the school and refuse to acknowledge the totalitarian power of the teacher. They don't have to go through the curriculum and don't have to take tests. Nothing is expected of them and all that is expected of their teachers is to get them off the backs of the rest of the staff in the school. Many extraordinary teachers have accepted this situation and created free and open classrooms for their "special" students. The main problem one has to worry about when such a class works well is whether by handling the school's problems one isn't indirectly helping the system by reducing conflicts created by the system itself.

Troubles with Students

Students are no more used to making choices and functioning in a free environment than their teachers are. We have all been taught to obey and be dependent, and breaking the habit of dependency is difficult. Consequently when one tries to develop an open classroom the students themselves will often be bewildered and frustrated at first. They will even at times insist that the teacher tell them what to do.

Last year I taught a special class in education at the University of California, Berkeley. The class was to be free and open, and the students could pursue whatever they wanted to. For the first three meetings members of the class sat around and bitched because I refused to tell them what to do. They wanted to know what I wanted them to do and since I had nothing in mind for them they were angry. I even got a sense that they felt rejected because they weren't directed. It took over a month for people to begin to look about and examine their school careers, sort out what they wanted to learn about and what they needed to forget. As it turned out, some students wanted to write poetry, others to study the high school curriculum, and most of the students wanted to find out about each other. We all realized that they had been at college for three or four years, sat in innumerable classes looking at their professors and never knew the people who sat next to them.

I considered my role in that class was to bring in things to share with the students and to be available to help them. I brought books and articles and poems to class, and left them there. Sometimes we talked about them though often we didn't. However, my bringing what I cared about to the class made it easier for them to bring things that were important to them.

One has to be patient with freedom and have as rich an environment as possible available for students so there will be things they can choose to do. One cannot ask pupils to be free or make choices in a vacuum. There is no limit to what can be brought to class to enrich the environment. A partial list would include:

—second-hand books
—old magazines
—scraps of wood, metal, and cloth discarded by factories
—old billboard posters
—parts of broken machines—cars, TVs, radios, toasters, etc.
—tape recorders and tape
—old toys
—old clothes to be used to create a classroom costume closet
—a sewing machine and needles and thread

—discarded advertising materials such as signs,
  posters, booklets, sales tags, handbills
—comfortable old furniture or rugs
—light fixtures, flashlights, wire, bulbs, batteries
—typewriters
—posters and buttons of all sorts

Children will use materials brought into the classroom and left around in the most unexpected ways.
Recently a friend offered me a ton of balsa wood to
use with my class and I readily accepted. He arrived
a few days later with three ocean liner life rafts cut
up in sections. Some were six feet long, others nine
and twelve feet. Many of the pieces were rounded
at the ends. He dumped the whole pile in the back
yard and showed me that beneath the canvas, the
life rafts were indeed made out of balsa wood and
glue in about equal proportions. The balsa wood was
not retrievable and in despair I just let the rafts lie
in the back yard for several months. One day several
of my students decided to paint the sections and
bring them into our room. After a few days all of
our chairs were replaced by the life rafts. They made
wonderful room dividers, seats, and tables. Also,
when piled on top of each other they made a cozy
little house or boat for the kids to play in. Every day
the rafts were used in different ways. The students
saw in those forms possibilities I had never imagined.

Being free enough to let the kids explore such
possibilities is not easy. As Zelda Wirtschafter, a
teacher with a good deal of experience in work with
open classrooms, has put it:

Helping teachers to understand that there is
nothing sacrosanct about the standard curriculum
outlines—and that providing children with the opportunity and resources to explore their own questions is far more important and valid a learning
experience than "covering" a paper sequence of
topics—is to my mind the overriding problem of
the day. My experience has been that once teachers
free themselves of the feeling that they "are not
teaching their kids anything," and learn to perceive
as real learning the activities and questions and
conversations which develop spontaneously in their
classrooms, they become much more confident and
relaxed and many of the former problems of control simply disappear.

On Student Teaching and Its Problems

Institutions that train teachers often play the role
of gatekeeper for the school system they service.
They give credentials to young people who seem
able to conform to the demands of the system and
deny them to potential troublemakers. The teachers
who are picked to supervise student teaching are
often the most confident and representative teachers
in a school system. Usually they have things well
under control in their classes and have easy authoritarian manners. They are not particularly oppressive if students obey, and they know how to deal
with defiant students. They have the curriculum
down pat and know just what to expect from their

class at every moment. Their students are quiet and industrious, their rooms are clean, and their routines work well. They are content with the way things are.

Student teachers are welcome in such classrooms and are expected to follow the example of these benevolent dictators. If the student teachers believe there ought to be another way of existing in the classroom, a freer and more student-centered way, their ideas will be received coldly and often hostilely. If the student teachers try to loosen things in the classroom they will often find themselves dismissed from student teaching and may find it difficult to get their credentials. Conflicts between student teachers and their supervising teachers are backed up by the staff of the training institution and so the defiant student teacher stands alone, just as the defiant child in school stands alone.

Yet one can't teach in public schools without credentials. It is a question of how much one can put up with, how much one is willing to compromise, and, finally, how badly one wants to teach. Many people find it easier to teach on provisional licenses that require a minimum of education credits, and go to school at night, than to make their way through a master's program that seems to them irrelevant. Still, for people who have gone through twelve years of elementary and secondary schooling and four years of college, another year of compliance needn't be devastating. What matters is the work that goes on within the schools. It may well be worth keeping cool until the credentials are in hand.

On Selecting a School for Your Training

If you can, pick a school of education that is small
and inconspicuous. Avoid large conservative institutions like Teachers College, Columbia, and the University of California, Berkeley. The big places are
likely to be more conventional than the smaller ones
and are likely to give less conventional, freer teachers a much more difficult time. The greater the
reputation an institution has to defend, the more
resistant it is to change. Schools of education that
consider themselves little more than "credential
factories" are more likely to let one through than
schools with a "philosophy." This may seem an excessively cynical view, yet it has been my experience
that very little of interest is happening in *any* school
of education and therefore if one wants credentials
one might as well get them in the easiest and least
painful way.

Tests as Cultural Documents

There are some demands that the school system makes upon students that one cannot get around. If all the pupils in a system must be tested for I.Q. or Reading Achievement, every teacher has to go along. If students want to attend college, they have to take College Board exams and if they want certain jobs they have to take Civil Service exams. Whatever one thinks of the testing system, young people have to live with some form of it. However, they needn't be defeated by tests nor need they be scared of the cold objective eye of the test-makers. Tests are cultural documents and are made by individuals who want specific answers to their questions. If one can look at a test as a symptom of the prevailing culture, devised by men of flesh and blood, who have moral and social reasons for asking the questions they do, it may be easier to cool the tests out and figure out what is expected. For example, if one realizes that test-makers usually want the simplest and not the cleverest of answers, since they are not interested in creativity as much as the ability to follow directions, one can avoid a lot of uncertainty and anxiety.

Students are not usually taught how to take tests. Rather they are challenged by tests which are treated as ritually sacred documents in the schools. I remember how the Reading Achievement tests in my school were dealt with. They came to the school wrapped in sealed paper and were put away in a safe. Then the instructions were sent to teachers who had to study them carefully and ultimately repeat each word of the directions to the students they were to test. The test couldn't be explained in a natural way. The directions had to be read. Moreover, teachers were not allowed to test their own classes. This might, as the jargon goes, destroy the objectivity of the instrument. The effect of this objectivity was to create an unfamiliar situation that caused a great deal of anxiety for my students. Not only did they have to deal with the test itself but also with a forbidding adult who read the directions aloud and looked out for cheaters.

Tests as documents and testers as people try to present themselves in as grave a manner as possible in order to underline their importance. If students can see through this solemnity for the sham performance it is they can treat tests with a sense of humor and maybe deal with them as necessary burdens rather than as mortal threats.

I found it useful to play test-maker with my students and have them assume that role, too. We talked about the kinds of questions one could ask if one cared to screen out troublemakers, radicals, creative people, energetic people, angry people, etc. We talked about the desirable traits from the point of view of the system of a teacher, a welfare worker, a college student. Then we looked at sample tests and analyzed the kinds of questions being asked. We parodied the questions and played with them. The students tested each other with mock solemnity and learned how not to be afraid of failing or passing tests. They learned, or at least some learned, how to confront tests without being victimized by them.

Evaluating Without Testing

Tests are made to measure one student against another student or to measure a student's performance against some standard which is to be expected of him. When a teacher abandons the notion that all students must live up to some given standards, or have their worth measured against the worth of other students, new means of evaluating a student's work must be developed. These other more qualitative means of evaluation are not difficult to imagine. One can consider first of all a student's work in relation to other work he has done. Then one can compare it to earlier work which the student has attempted or achieved (a complex question which may involve talking at length with the student and perhaps with other adults who know the student's work). The work can also be considered in relation to specific models, from art, science, or literature, that the student knows or tries to use, or in relation to the issue the student is dealing with, or the thought or feeling he is attempting to communicate. Last, the work can be considered in relation to the work of other students, to what they attempted, and can be of use to the student in question. Evaluation should look ahead to future work as well as deal with the quality of any particular effort.

For example, a junior high school student of mine recently wrote a poem ("School Is a Figment of the Imagination," page 105). This was the first completed poem she showed me. The rest of her work was influenced by Tolkien's *Fellowship of the Ring* and was filled with dragons, knights, elves, and other fantastical creatures. The writing was clever, and yet she seemed to lose interest in her own tales and poems and never finished them. I was struck by how different this poem was and told her my feelings. We talked about her old style and she said that reading Emmett Williams' *Anthology of Concrete Poetry* gave her the idea for the poem. We talked for a while about the shapes of poems and their relationships with the meaning of the words in a poem. Then we talked about school, about her hatred of school, about ideal schools and real schools. Then we talked about her work, where it could go, and why it seemed so incomplete before. Then I suggested she write about her ideal school, and she did:

The School that Ought to Be

The school that ought to be has teachers that know how to handle their classes (keep them interested) and know *what they are teaching*.

Subjects:

Pleasurable* Human Behavior
*for the people you behave to and yourself
Historydrama
Naturemath
Creative Cookery (on a Budget)

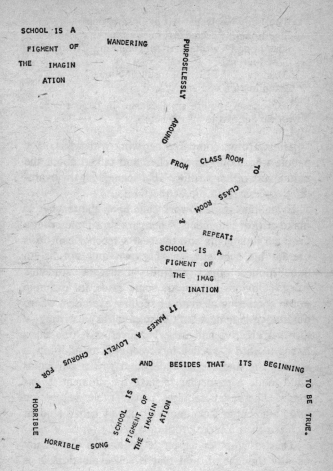

SCHOOL IS A FIGMENT OF THE IMAGINATION WANDERING PURPOSELESSLY AROUND FROM CLASS ROOM TO CLASS ROOM. REPEAT: SCHOOL IS A FIGMENT OF THE IMAGINATION IT MAKES A LOVELY CHORUS FOR A HORRIBLE HORRIBLE SONG AND BESIDES THAT ITS BEGINNING TO BE TRUE.

HA!

— Michaele Lundberg

> The Long-Neglected Art of Observation
> The Long-Neglected Art of Walking
> The Long-Neglected Art of Thinking Clearly
> (Meditation)
> Mastery of the Elegant Insult (optional)
> Examination of Fantasy
>
> These classes require small classes in large rooms
> with easy access to everywhere.

Afterward we compared her work with what other people were doing in the class and talked about the uniqueness of her writing. That seemed all the evaluation necessary to me at the time.

Evaluating student work calls upon the teacher to make critical judgments. There are no simple criteria for such judgments and the best a teacher can do is present his evaluation as his own and not as an unquestioned objective truth about the student's work. (Obviously there are some cases, for example, in the correcting of math or spelling exercises, where qualitative judgment isn't as relevant as in writing or in other creative activities. However, it is one thing to say a word is spelled incorrectly or an addition is wrong, and another to understand why a particular child made a particular mistake the moment it was made. The latter requires considerable perception and judgment and can more effectively help a student to learn than a mere cross or a zero.)

There is another aspect to evaluation that is not usually thought of, and that is self-evaluation. It is not only important for teachers to judge the work of their students; they should also evaluate their own work—where they helped or misled their students, or where they were exciting or irrelevant.

Teachers rarely talk to one another about their work or reflect on it themselves. They depend upon teachers' manuals and supervisors and experts for evaluation of their work and for resources. It shouldn't be that way. One ought to examine one's own work, perhaps by keeping an anecdotal diary that can be looked over every week or so. More than that one ought to find other teachers with whom one can share one's experience and to whom one can talk freely of success and failure in the classroom.

The failure of teachers is generally concealed in the life of schools. Yet a major way teachers can learn to be more effective with young people is through facing their failures, and making fresh starts. Supervisors treat the failures of teachers in the same way as teachers are supposed to treat student failures. The teacher is blamed for his failure and is left to correct it in the isolation of his own classroom. We have to move beyond the competitive judging of one another's work and support one another, share experiences, and develop a community of teachers within the school who can relate to one another openly and honestly.

On Correcting

The poet and teacher John Hollander said at a meeting on the teaching of writing that the act of correcting a child's work can be an act of love. In a review published in the *Urban Review* he elaborated on the theme:

> . . . to make the act of correction . . . more like a caress than a blow is one of the axioms of teaching the young. And if one is to believe that we are now faced with generations of pupils for whom anything like a caress feels like an act of violence, then the problem is to discover the appropriate gesture upon which the tactical rhetoric of correction will be based.

It is not a matter of whether one corrects a student's paper so much as a question of when and how. Students produce some papers that they care about and others that they would just as soon forget. In school, teachers have a tendency to consider all the work of a student on the same level. Everything a student does is supposed to be a finished product. There is little allowance for hesitant beginnings, false starts, bad ideas, impossible dreams—all the explorations writers attempt before finding their own voices and the forms appropriate to expressing them. They are expected to be perfect every time. In my experience when students produce a work they care about they want it to be correct in every way—that is, to communicate as fully as possible. They ask for corrections and want to get things right.

To be open does not mean that one must accept everything students do by any means. We have a uniform spelling for our language, for example, and it is a disservice to pupils to ignore the matter of spelling altogether. However, after a teacher tells his students the way things are (and usually, though not always, there are sane reasons for present conventions), it is up to the students themselves to decide how they want to deal with these conventions. Once they know about the rules of uniform spelling, they should be free to accept or modify them as they please. The rules of spelling are no more universal and objective than the results of I.Q. and Achievement Tests.

Reporting to Parents, Students, and Supervisors

Document what is happening in your class.
Document what you are trying to do.
Let the students' work speak for the students.
Do not be afraid to admit that you have blundered.
Show people what is happening in your classroom, tell them what you are trying to do. Talk about education, learning, young people. When parents ask what is happening to their children let them see their children's work, talk about their children as indi-

viduals. Put everything on a personal and qualitative level.

Reporting is fighting for survival. If you care and let people know you care, you may survive. There is no guarantee.

VIII
Conclusions

How Long Does It Take?

Recently a teacher asked me how long it took to work out more open ways of teaching. She asked for an estimate of days and weeks. She was trying to develop a freer classroom and experienced bad days and good days. There were times when her pupils knew what they wanted to do and worked hard and well. There were other times of hostility, silence, and occasionally violence. She experienced impatience herself—felt nervous when some of her pupils relaxed and contented themselves with talking to each other, or came late, or invited friends to her class. She was afraid that the students weren't learning anything and felt defensive when facing supervisors or other teachers. Her main problem, however, was struggling with the environment of her classroom. She didn't know what to offer students, and while she struggled with making her classroom a sane place to be in, she was bombarded by demands from the school administration and her own conscience. She had to fill in forms, give tests, take attendance, assign monitors, go to fire drills, listen for bells, read the principal's daily bulletin, and still worry about her students and their lives. Her conscience demanded that she know what her pupils were doing every moment they spent in her class even though her philosophy told her that it was neither important nor possible to know what students were learning at any given time.

She also made mistakes with her students that she regretted. She told them at the beginning of the year that she trusted them, yet kept a close eye on her pocketbook. She let them leave the room if they cared to, yet worried that they would get into trouble and worse, would get her into trouble. She gave her students choices, including the choice not to do something and yet was disappointed when they exercised their options. Often despite her philosophy she took back the freedom she offered to her class and insisted they shut up or do an assignment. She regretted her outbursts of frustration, yet telling the students of her regrets seemed to make matters worse. The more she confided her confusion to her students the more they moved away from her. It wasn't that they didn't like her—more likely they distrusted her uncertainty. In many ways it was more dangerous because less predictable than a simple totalitarian attitude.

This teacher's tale was familiar. It described what I went through the first time I taught. For me the first six months were a disaster. I wanted my class to be open and my students to do what was interesting to them. Yet the demands the system made upon me were overwhelming. Worse, however, was my inability to develop an environment in which my students could discover things that interested them. It took me at least a year to feel comfortable in a school environment and know young people well enough to present them with options for learning which might prove meaningful to them.

But six months were not enough—after six months of chaos I experienced at least six months of groping and getting to understand students as people and not merely as pupils. It took at least a year for me to be at ease in my classroom and to stop worrying about what was supposed to happen and start reacting directly to what was actually happening. Nothing developed magically; freedom and openness are not formulas for success, and it is very difficult indeed to explore the diverse possibilities of life in schools. To have a free classroom is to present an environment where many people can discover themselves, and there is no simple set of rules to prescribe how this can be created.

It is almost certain that open classrooms will not develop within our school systems without the teachers and pupils experiencing fear, depression, and panic. There will always be the fear that one is wrong in letting people choose their own lives instead of legislating their roles in society. There will be depression, for one can never know in the short range if one is succeeding in opening possibilities to people or merely deceiving and seducing them. And there will be panic because we all fear chaos—fear that things have gotten so far out of hand in our lives that if we face the truth we will no longer be able to tolerate life.

Our schools are crazy. They do not serve the interests of adults, and they do not serve the interests of young people. They teach "objective" knowledge and its corollary, obedience to authority. They teach avoidance of conflict and obeisance to tradition in the guise of history. They teach equality and democracy while castrating students and controlling teachers. Most of all they teach people to be silent about what they think and feel, and worst of all, they teach people to pretend that they are saying what they think and feel. To try to break away from stupid schooling is no easy matter for teacher or student. It is a lonely and long fight to escape from believing that one needs to do what people say one should do and that one ought to be the person one is expected to be. Yet to make such an escape is a step toward beginning again and becoming the teachers we never knew we could be.

Notes

Readers may want to use this space to keep notes on classroom experiences and other observations as they relate to *The Open Classroom*. Both the author and the publisher will be interested in comments from those who have read and made use of this book; these should be sent to Box OC, *The New York Review of Books*, 250 West 57th Street, New York City, N.Y. 10019.

NOTES

NOTES

NOTES

NOTES

NOTES

NOTES

NOTES

HERBERT R. KOHL is the author of *The Age of Complexity* (Mentor Books), *36 Children* (New American Library), and the pamphlet *Teaching the "Unteachable"* (New York Review). Mr. Kohl received his bachelor's degree in philosophy from Harvard and a master's degree in special education from Teachers College, Columbia, and was a Henry Fellow at Oxford in philosophy. Formerly on the staff of the center for Urban Education and director of the Teachers and Writers Collaborative at the Horace Mann-Lincoln Institute of School Experimentation, he taught for several years in Harlem schools. He has recently been director of an experimental program in the Berkeley schools, called "Other Ways."